The
BOOK
of JOB

The
BOOK
of JOB

With Commentary
by Thomas Moore

RIVERHEAD BOOKS, NEW YORK

Riverhead Books
Published by The Berkley Publishing Group
A member of Penguin Putnam Inc.
200 Madison Avenue
New York, New York 10016

First Riverhead edition: March 1998

The Peguin Putnam World Wide Web site address is
http://www.penguinputnam.com

The Library of Congress Cataloging-in-Publication Data

Bible. O.T. Job. English. Authorized. 1998.
   The Book of Job / with commentary by Thomas Moore.—1st
Riverhead ed.
     p.   cm.
  ISBN 1-57322-674-2
  1. Bible. O.T. Job—Commentaries. I. Moore, Thomas. 1940– .
II. Title.
BS1413.M59   1998
223'.1077—dc21   97-45166
                                              CIP

Printed in the United States of America

10 9 8 7 6 5 4 3 2 1

PREFACE

The Riddle

One of the most sublime pieces of literature from the ancient world, The Book of Job could have been written yesterday, both because of its post-modern structure, which may or may not be due to eons of editing and textual corruption, and because it addresses a theme of crucial relevance to our time. It is sometimes said that the story as we have it is a patchwork of editors, but I appreciate its form nonetheless. Its disjunctions and inconsistencies mirror human emotion and thought. I trust it more with its odd turns than I would were it smooth and logical.

Because it ends with the happy restoration of Job's children and possessions, the renowned literary critic Northrop Frye describes The Book of Job as comedy, at least in the technical sense. But I see it as a true comic jewel, in the full meaning of the word comedy. Most religions turn to parables, jokes, paradoxes, and sometimes even buffoonery to express the most serious and profound truths, and I'm sure that a good dramatist could present Job in all its dark humor and stinging irony.

More specifically, the story presents itself as an implicit riddle. A sacred riddle is an obscure, playful question, the answer to which gives the key to life. The famous riddle of the Sphinx—What has four legs in the morning, two in the afternoon, and three in the evening—was not just a teasing puzzle. If you didn't guess the right answer—a human being, who crawls in infancy, walks in maturity, and uses a cane in old age—your life was at stake, because the sphinx would devour you. And it's true: If you don't realize the scope of your human life and see it as a piece, you don't really live. If you don't understand that the meaning of life is a riddle, you may pursue it too earnestly and find your way into tragedy.

What is the riddle of Job? We will be able to answer that question only after reflecting on the story closely. Obviously, it has to do with the role of suffering in human life, perhaps the most difficult mystery of all. Specifically, it asks why the innocent suffer—a real challenge to the person who believes in the essential goodness of life or who hasn't yet come to appreciate the complexity of the cosmic design.

For almost twenty years I worked as a psychotherapist, sitting hour after hour with people looking for explanations for their suffering. Whether they were going through a divorce, dealing with the loss of a loved one, facing cancer, consumed with the desire to kill themselves, or simply longing to lose weight or gain weight or quit smoking or have satisfying sex— in all these cases they usually came with the question: Why is this happening to me?

They believed that if they could answer this one question, their suffering might be relieved completely, as if by magic, or at least it would become bearable. Like most modern people, they trusted their rationality. If only they could understand, if only they could pinpoint a cause, if only they could place the blame, then they could get on with life. If suffering makes sense, they believed, then it could be borne.

All those hours of therapy were nothing less than a re-enactment of The Book of Job, a frustrated search for reasons and explanations carried out while some other process was in play. Most of my clients wanted answers, preferably from me. I sat there thinking that this wish for an accounting for misery was part of their problem. The more important challenge might be not how to make sense of suffering, but how to live when life is empty, wounded, or miserable.

This question seems to me more fruitful than the usual posing of Job's dilemma: Why does a just person suffer? We may have to consider this mystery of innocent suffering along the way, but as many popular psychologists have warned, the "why" question gets us nowhere. I remember many hours of therapy in which a person would present an explanation for why they were suffering. By the end of the hour, the explanation had been discussed quite thoroughly, but it left us feeling empty and unresolved. Sometimes, the next week the person would present an altogether new explanation with fresh enthusiasm and hope, only to find the familiar emptiness and dissatisfaction. Over the years, I became convinced that the thoughtful deepening of the question was the surest route to whatever it is one looks for in therapy.

For me, therapy began to make progress, which I must admit was actually a kind of fruitful regression, when we both forgot the original question, when it passed into oblivion or, as Emily Dickinson would say, when it became absorbed. In that case, therapy is like Zen sitting—a forgetting of the project at hand so that the question you didn't have the presence of mind to ask comes to the fore. Our stated questions are usually—I'd like to say always—a defense against the soul that tries to make itself visible and wants tending. As psychoanalysis says, intellectual inquiry can be a form of defense. As I've tried to emphasize in all of my writing, care of the soul is the point, not satisfaction of the mind or the modification of behavior.

I'm using therapy as a model here for all of living. Job is not about therapy, but I've encountered him there. In every aspect of life we ask the question "Why?" or "Who is to blame?" or

"Did I do something wrong?" Job's challenge is: How do I go on? How do I find it in myself to have a necessary modicum of hope and optimism? What can I say that would make any difference? This is the riddle of Job, and it is indeed a riddle, because once we find the answer we can laugh, and our laughter will be the sign of our incipient hope.

From my late teens I've enjoyed the writings of Samuel Beckett because he writes in the spirit of Job. He sidesteps the rational explanations and reasons for living, instead showing our own hopelessness as human beings. Outrageously he sketches the comic nature of the human condition, comic even in the very heart of suffering. We laugh at Krapp, who finds his entire life a pile of dung. We laugh at Vladimir and Estragon as they wait eternally for Godot, whose presence presumably will give them a reason for living. Ironically, the very emptiness in their waiting gives their lives something of a point. We laugh at Murphy whom Beckett describes as sitting naked in his rocking chair, out of the sunlight, tied to his post by seven scarves—a graphic, symbolic image of human bondage.

My own life feels much like that of a Beckett character. At thirteen I left the warm comforts of a loving family to enter the cool world of monasticism. I struggled to stay with that life for twelve years, thinking all the time that all the deprivation and coldness would be worth the effort once I was ordained a priest. Then, six months before the planned ordination, something possessed me to leave. I've never regretted leaving that life and abandoning that goal, but still it's difficult to find meaning for all those years. Then I sought a career in music, which I loved. But the career never came to pass. I worked hard to get a Ph.D. in religion so I could spend the rest of my days teaching in a small college, where I thought

I'd have like-minded colleagues and appreciative students. I found a position at a large university, but because of my interests or style of teaching and writing, I felt profoundly misunderstood and rejected. After a few years, they told me to leave, leaving me in the cold once again to find my way in life.

Over the years I've been in and out of deep and promising relationships, only to have them end with pain and the failure of understanding on all sides. My friend James Hillman once quite properly introduced me before I gave a lecture as someone who was not a scholar, not an artist, not a speaker, not a writer—not anything definable. His point was a positive and constructive one, but this condition of not fitting in, which I felt long before Hillman's accurate description, felt disorienting and lacking in meaning.

For several years in my late forties, I knew I had something to say and to give, but every college I approached told me there was no place for me. In the end, I would go to a small New England town library and tack up a notice that I was looking for students, and six or seven would appear. I remember one night in western Massachusetts giving a talk on myth and meaning to about twelve people in a small library conference room. I made a grand gesture, and the single floor lamp that lit the room fell over and the lightbulb smashed into pieces. I felt this slight mishap as a sign of where I had come with all my learning and promise—the light gone out, scattered in pieces around my feet.

Even now I wonder why it took me fifty years to find my life, to be able to be married, to know what it is to love one's own children, to have a home that I can feel is my own. When I lived in rented houses in the Berkshires, an owner might decide at a whim that she would like to live in "my" house, and I would be sent packing. It happened more than once. In those days, I once suggested to a psychoanalytic institute that I could give a seminar on the therapeutic use of dreams, and they laughed at my audacity.

These trials are simple compared to more devastating experiences of many people, and yet they represent a truth that affects everyone's life to one degree or another. Some are disillusioned by life's failure to please and are distressed by the sensation of being abnormal or unsuccessful. When they see their friends' achievements, they feel a deep and debilitating envy. When they first sense failure, they protect themselves by taking on a harsh cynical attitude that gradually becomes habitual and life-defining. They take failure literally and don't see the comedy in it. They can't laugh at themselves and give up out of disillusionment.

Job presents us with the riddle that everyone is challenged to answer, and in this sense Job is everybody and everybody is Job. How can life make sense when it never seems to work out as planned or hoped? A quick glance at the world gives the sure impression that the wicked prosper and the good suffer. It seems true, too, that the wishes we harbor for years, when fulfilled, sometimes turn out to be empty if not positively destructive.

Why do many people turn to spiritual leaders, who often take advantage of them and make them into passive followers? Why do many people keep reading the latest self-help authors? Why do people flock to growth centers and watch television programs that offer emotional salvation? Because we have not yet taken to heart the lesson of Job, whose puzzling story questions the widely held assumption that life is a problem to be solved.

Job's friends try to make him realize that his suffering is due to his sinful life. Today, we wouldn't use the word sin. We would say: You eat the wrong foods. You don't relax or exercise. You are overweight, stressed, too sedate. The voices of Job's accusers are as loud and clear today as they ever were. They have no time for riddles, so sincere and so earnest is their attempt to figure out the ups and downs of a life.

But in the Bible, Job stays with the riddle until he finds his way out and is restored. This is his secret: He doesn't fall for the reasonable interpretations and advice he gets from his friends. He speaks out of his confusion, even when he feels his words are out of place and maybe blasphemous. He doesn't sustain an argument or follow a line of reasoning or ever come up with a satisfying explanation. He remains true to the reactions of his soul. He sees his situation not as a problem to be solved but as his riddle to ponder. Like Oedipus before the Sphinx, his destiny in his hands, he presents a particular myth about suffering and self-possession.

The Myth

A myth is a particular kind of story that plays a crucial role in the lives of individuals and communities. In the modern world, we are accustomed to thinking of reality as a collection of facts and events, and accordingly we're absorbed with information and analysis. We have bracketed out the idea that our very interest in facts and events is part of a story that shapes our lives and accounts for the things we do and the ways we understand ourselves and our world.

When a scientist tells us how the world works, information comes to the foreground and narrative slides into the shadows.

The story doesn't disappear—we simply don't think about what we're doing as having anything to do with a story. We lose the distance between fact and reflection that a sense of story would provide, and so we tend to take our facts literally. In this worldview, we look for explanations for behavior and feeling in the facts of our upbringing, our chemical makeup, and the genes that we assume account for all aspects of body and soul.

We may not be conscious of the stories we live, but nevertheless we are always caught up in a narrative of some kind. The stories may not be complete and may not correspond to any that we have heard told, yet the story contributes significantly to who we are and what we do. Once in a while we may catch a glimpse of the stories we're living out in bits of conversation or in an impressive dream, but for the most part we remain locked inside our stories, taking them literally. Another way to understand therapy is to see it as bringing to light the narratives we're living.

You could say that there are two kinds of myth or two meanings for the word: the story we live and the stories we tell. We need to tell stories to know what stories we're living—not so much to understand the stories but to be closer to them, aware of them, and less identified with them. The unexamined life is indeed not worth living because our tendency is to live out a collective story without the individuality and choice that reflection affords. Telling, reading, and listening to stories educates the imagination, preparing us to live in tune with narratives that make life meaningful.

Mythic stories depict the deepest and most formative themes of human life, and since they transcend details of personality and individuality, they are usually not strong on these points.

Myth paints with a broad brush. It is also not bound by unities of time and place or the necessities of nature. Myth may be filled with fantastic beings and events, and the facts may be symbolic and allegorical rather than literal. But one should not be misled into thinking that the fantastic nature of a myth means that the story is not important or significant to human life. On the contrary, no story is more relevant than myth to the deepest issues a person has to face. For all its fanciful imagery, nothing is closer to the truth.

All this is prelude to suggesting that the story of Job is a myth that dramatically and poetically describes the devastating loss of happiness and the advent of serious suffering in a human life. A philosopher would offer reasonable reflections on this theme, while myth depicts the full drama, complete with a wide range of emotions, the personification of conflicting attitudes, and the grand, cosmic context in which such a profound question has to be explored.

Myth takes us to the realm of the gods, goddesses, and other divine beings, so that we can glimpse the backgrounds of human conflict. The tale of Job is no exception, as it begins with the wager made in heaven that sets everything in motion. Satan, or the Adversary, convinces Yahweh to test Job's loyalty. When he's prospering, of course he will be faithful, but give him some real trouble, and then we'll find out how deep his faith lies. The reader is aware of the narrative behind Job's suffering, but Job is not.

The story is about a test of Job's constancy, but let us not take the notion of test literally. It is possible, especially in times of unusual ordeal and struggle, to *imagine* life as a test. This is one way among many to picture our circumstances. "Test" is an archetypal image of the human condition, and if we imagine our situation as a test, we will respond in certain ways. We talk about some situations as trials and ordeals, wondering if we'll measure up to our own expectations and those of others. But there is also an absolute judge, the sense that life itself tests our mettle and uncovers what we're made of.

Any struggle can be seen as a test, which may intensify the drama in our situation. An actual court trial can be the most serious experience of a lifetime, and yet at the same time it is highly dramatic and of deep interest. Why else would movies and television programs use the trial form so frequently and so successfully? We find pleasure in trials and tests. In most cases, fictional court trials turn out the way we want them to, and therefore take the form of comedy in the classical sense. Magazines often reduce complex issues to tests. People enjoy taking tests to discover their proper weight, the risk of heart disease, their life expectancy, or their chances in love.

The story of Job places human suffering within the context of a test in which Job will be judged according to his response. Although the form of test can have a certain degree of pleasure, it can also be the source of excruciating anxiety, as anyone who has gone to school knows. The fact that there is an entire genre of dreams that take the form of a test or examination, dreams typically loaded with anxiety, tells us how deeply this archetypal form touches us.

As the ones being tested, we take the role of the masochist and those giving the test risk falling into severe forms of sadism. Students can suffer profoundly when they enter the role too passively, and teachers can become cruel unconsciously and in spite of their constructive ideas about education. Job endures several degrees of suffering: his business, family, and personal losses; the test of his character and faithfulness; and the taunts of his friends, whose comforting takes the form of harsh interpretation of his life and bitter advice. The framework of ordeal, announced at the outset of the story, makes everything that follows more painful.

Perceiving life as a test, we may enter deep into the role of masochist and find no job or pleasure anywhere in life. It isn't unusual for people to feel habitually that they don't measure up. They may interpret this testing in literal ways, believing that they have been brought up needing to please their mother or father, authority figures, or a spouse, and certainly these personalities may play a role at a certain level of suffering. But Job transcends the personal level where life may be a literal ordeal and reveals its mythic or archetypal depth. Our feeling of being tested, whoever it is we imagine giving the test, lies deep in the narrative by which we live.

The way out of this particular kind of suffering is not to try to avoid it, but to go right into it. It's a fact that we are victims of fate. At any time, an accident or illness or some other development might change our lives and bring unexpected suffering. We are at the mercy of time, culture, family, even love. But we have the choice either to live with a controlling ego, where we feel we must understand ourselves and our world, or to submit to a greater design that we don't understand and over which we have little control. In the latter case, we may have to be profoundly present to and speak from our pain.

The first way leads to a fully secular life and is represented by modern culture, which uses all its resources for understanding and control. Our cultural idea of a successful future is to be able to control the weather and overcome death and illness. Other societies may take a religious attitude and live in sympathy—a traditional word—with fate and the demands of nature. These cultures rely on magic, art, and religion for security and creativity.

Because we think we can control nature and can overlook fate and destiny as elements in our personal lives, we also blame ourselves when illness and other misfortunes appear. This kind of guilt feeling and guilt making is simply an aspect of our secular style of living. Interestingly, this is the point of view represented by Eliphaz, Bildad, and Zophar, Job's friendly tormentors. They insist that Job is responsible for his suffering because he is a sinful man. "Who ever perished being innocent?" they ask.

Initially Job responds to misfortune with a basic, unconditional religious affirmation of life: "The Lord gave, and the Lord hath taken away. Blessed be the name of the Lord." Then, as his friends try to correct what they see as a simplistic point of view, his religious attitude deepens. Some commentators see Job's response as inconsistent, and they suppose that the text must be corrupted, that we don't have a complete story. To me, Job is simply being human in his response. He praises God and then he goes through an initiation into a deeper appreciation of what it means to be religious. His sardonic friends help him find his way through the complexities entailed by his fundamental religious affirmation and faith.

Eliphaz, Bildad, and Zophar remind me of tempters in another ancient tale of initiation—the story of Eros and Psyche. In this myth, Psyche begins as a naive young woman looking for love. When she finds love in the person of Eros himself, she is asked to be with him in darkness so that she'll never see exactly who it is she loves. Her sisters are jealous of her and tempt her to break her promise to remain in darkness by lighting an oil lamp in the middle of the night. They tell her that her lover is actually a beast who doesn't want to be seen for who he is. Eventually, Psyche gives in to their taunts and brings a light to their bedroom. Eros wakes up and immediately departs. There follow several ordeals by which Psyche loses her naiveté before she is finally reunited with her lover.

Job's friends are like Psyche's sisters. They seem annoying and self-serving, and yet they help Job deepen his religious attitude. He doesn't give in to them literally, but they intensify the drama in which Job makes his way toward a less innocent faithfulness. In our own lives these friendly tempters may be sensed internally as voices or attitudes that counter our fundamental trust in life. We get sick, and we ask: "What have I done to deserve this? If only I had lived differently, if only I had taken better care of myself, if only I were different." Job says: "Let the day perish wherein I was born."

The tempters also find a voice in our actual friends and relatives who ask or tell us what we've done wrong. People commonly assume that a person can't be innocent and suffer at the same time. Experts from several disciplines tell us today that we suffer because of trauma in childhood, bad parenting, faulty genes, poverty, lack of education, or the failure of medical science to evolve quickly enough. They are all taking the role of Eliphaz, Bildad, and Zophar. Apparently they can't stand unexplained suffering. In our secular world it's difficult to find support for a religious response to suffering.

Job's "comforters" offer some subtle reasons for abandoning one's fundamental trust in life. Eliphaz says: "Happy is the man whom God correcteth: therefore despise not thou the chastening of the Almighty." This is the idea that suffering is a learning experience. If we're smart enough, we'll come away from it with new information that will make life better. Suffering is redeemed in the lessons we absorb.

It's true, sometimes we can learn a great deal from suffering and loss, but what about those many misfortunes that are truly tragic—the loss of a loved one, a terminal illness, a serious accident. Do we really want to reduce such tragedy to a learning experience? Job's response is to become inconsolably depressed. "Is there any taste in the white of an egg?" He considers suicide: "What is my end that I should prolong my life?" He enters deep into his hopelessness: "What is my strength that I should hope?" If Job were admitted to a hospital, which is quite likely if he were living today, he would probably be diagnosed as depressed and treated accordingly. But the Biblical story of his ordeal provides an alternative to treatment.

As myth, The Book of Job invites us to consider the necessity of depression, thoughts of suicide, and hopelessness. Here they are not clinical syndromes but elements in Job's initiation. Nor would I call them stages in his grief. Who knows if depression will ever lift or if hope will ever be restored. Suicide is often more than a thought—people kill themselves every day. Formulating Job's responses as stages toward ultimate health would misread the dramatic form of the Biblical narrative. The fantasy of normal development lies in the modern practice of lining up human emotions on a progressive grid. This way of imagining suffering is a rationalization, similar to the idea that all is redeemable if only we learn from the experience. Suffering is meaningful, we think, if it has a successful outcome or if it's only a phase in a process of personal growth.

Bildad gives Job the simplistic advice you can read in magazines today in slightly different language: "He is green before the sun." Just do the right and healthy thing, and your life will be full of sunshine—happiness, we call it. In recent times especially, our culture seems hell-bent on finding happiness through appropriate behavior. What else could be motivating people to run, grimacing and flushed, down bicycle lanes than to be fit and have healthy hearts? We want to avoid the suffering we see in the lives of friends and in our community.

There is nothing wrong with living a healthy life and avoiding illness, but a life defined by avoidance is not a very positive thing. I've heard researchers say that a person should be married and live close to their extended family because they will live longer. Is that a good reason for being a spouse or for being intimate with one's family, so that one can live longer? Quite properly Job becomes frustrated with these beguiling interpretations and recommendations. They make sense at a superficial level, but they also suck away our humanity, and they have no religion in them. They represent pure, secular prudence. I would like to believe that life is of greater proportions than can be explained by these simple cause-and-effect, narcissistically self-absorbed philosophies.

In response to Bildad, Job refers to God's power over nature. He is one who "commandeth the sun, and it riseth not." Here a crucial theme in the Job paradigm comes into the foreground —the sublime and awesome grandeur of creation. In the face of this vast mystery, how could we ever prove our innocence? Our lives are nothing compared to the infinity of life and the sublimity of God. The shadow side of this realization of nature's awesomeness is the human feeling that we are being toyed with. You give me a beautiful life, and then you reveal your plan to take it all away, Job complains. Just give me a moment's peace, he says, because this kind of life isn't worth living.

Zophar rubs the point in and lays on the classic guilt trip. Who could ever claim utter innocence? he says, echoing Job but with a different meaning to his words. We all do things we regret, and a good portion of life is given over to remorse. We have our learning experiences, and then we go on to contradict our own wisdom. We fail, we betray, and we do stupid things. If we're going to be treated by life as we live, then most of us are in for a tough time of it.

Now Job makes an interesting turn. He acknowledges that only God knows anything. Job knows nothing, and yet he wants to speak. "Let me alone, that I may speak, and let come on me what will." We begin to sense a deeper faith in Job as he abandons some of his earlier masochism and passivity. He praises God's wisdom, acknowledging his own ignorance, but then he demands to be heard.

At one time in my younger years, I was feeling unusually confused about how to deal with mortality. The issue came to a head for me just after I had read about the Buddhist acceptance of death as part of life, and then read Dylan Thomas's famous poem written on the occasion of his father's death: "Do Not Go Gentle Into That Good Night." Which is right? I asked myself and a few friends. Should we accept death, or should we fight it? Should we bow down before life's mystery and the awesomeness of immeasurable time and space, or should we gather up our puny lives and selves and speak strongly on our own behalf, almost in defiance of that sublime life that we love? Over the years and influenced by much reading I resolved the issue the way I think Job does—by living the tension of the weakness of our position and the strength of our voice.

Our lives don't amount to much, but we can speak loudly and be a presence on this earth for the few moments that we're given. There is no good reason to go on in a corrupt world in which fate is capricious, but we will go on just because we have a sliver of life in us. Let the doctors condemn us as beyond cure. Let the psychiatrists tell us we'll never be normal. Let the marriages come and go, as love remains elusive and out of reach. In all misfortune we can still find a human voice or a simple breath. Religious faith requires every ounce of resistance and every breath of acquiescence.

Job's friends accuse him of not having faith, and yet their point of view lacks all religion. This, too, is a paradox in our own time. Religious trust in life is found only through openness to fate, a love of life, a tolerance for human limitation and imperfection, and an embrace of the complexities of ethical living. Even so, religious institutions often, if not typically, speak in the manner of Eliphaz, Bildad, and Zophar. They lay on guilt, they emphasize sin, they see a quid pro quo between living according to the rules and finding success in life. They mouth the platitudes of religion but they don't always manifest a heart open to the mystery.

Job finds his voice in the midst of his nothingness, while religious institutions usually speak proudly from their vast resources. Many people, I suspect, live out the story of Job in their relationship to their church or their spiritual leaders, and in some cases, I'm sure, with their analysts, therapists, and physicians. The person who has lost health, love, or possessions has no substance from which to speak except his or her fundamental humanity. This, of course, is sufficient, but it takes great faith in one's own life to find the needed security there.

Like anyone in a state of crisis, Job vacillates between courage and faintheartedness. He stumbles into a common palliative wish that is soothing but not very satisfying. He longs for the return of a golden age when his life was full of success and honor, when God was his protector and not his tormentor. C. G. Jung refers to this temptation as the "regressive restoration of the persona," an attempt to go back to a way of life that seems now, at least, to have been comfortable and desirable.

Today, politicians like to talk about the good old days, when marriages held together and families remained intact. I've known men and women in therapy, who, when faced with profound change, attempted to restore a former idealized condition. Sometimes a spouse, having separated or even divorced, will go back into the marriage with the hope of conjuring up the golden age. A disillusioned, out-of-luck wanderer may return to a former career, thinking that the former life was better than the present one.

But there are problems with the fantasy of restoring a wonderful past. First, the past was never quite as good as it now appears to have been. In the United States, who would want to go back to gangsters, thoughtless pollution, undisturbed racism, McCarthyism and blacklisting, and cruel labor practices—to name a few fundamental blotches on our history. Our personal past, too, may not have been as blissful as our active, filtering memory might paint it.

Besides, we're attached to the present, too. We could get rid of automobiles that are polluting our air and crowding our streets and return to the horse and buggy, but we don't want to give up our conveniences. We could keep televisions out of our houses and return to the days of neighborhoods and friends and dancing and making live music at home. Some of us do practice this kind of regression, but television continues to infect American life with a low level of entertainment and discussion. Instead of merely retreating in fantasy into a gilded past, we could bring elements of that past into our present lives.

One of the more annoying and yet potentially liberating aspects of a Job-like catastrophe is the feeling of being dumb. Job sees himself as someone who once enjoyed honor and prestige, but now he has become the object of ridicule. Where once he enjoyed honor, now he is vilified. Where once he seemed to be wise, now he is a fool.

The tradition of the "holy fool" has a special place in religious thought, although the idea is sometimes treated sentimentally. To be open to greater vision, the religious traditions teach, we have to become ignorant in a certain sense. Psychologically, too, it can be helpful to have our pet ideas seriously questioned. In small ways the feeling of foolishness might appear regularly in anyone's life, and once in a while the fool may descend with his full weight. The more public and exalted our displays of wisdom, the more crushing the visitations of the holy fool can be. I don't like the appearance of the fool in my life, but at a distance I can appreciate how important it is for my humanity to be relieved of my supposed wisdom and certainties.

I speak of the fool as holy to distinguish this archetype from the literal experience of being a fool or playing the fool. It's one thing to be literally foolish and another to feel the figure of the fool do his important work of desecularizing consciousness. This subtle fool is holy because he wipes away, at least momentarily, the sensation of understanding things that ought to remain mysterious. The fool plays an important role in the deepening of religious sensibility, which I take to be the central theme of The Book of Job.

The Voice

Finally, after Job's initiation into holy foolishness, the voice of God speaks from out of a whirlwind or tempest. It is a mighty, terrible voice that humbles Job even further. It is a voice that speaks for the grandeur and power of creation in contrast to the puniness of human life. God emphasizes the great beasts, Behemoth and Leviathan among them, over whom human beings have no power, and he describes the vastness of nature: "Canst thou bind the sweet influences of Ple'-ia-des, or loose the bands of O-ri'-on?" the Voice asks Job tauntingly.

In response, Job admits: "Therefore have I uttered that I understood not; things too wonderful for me, which I knew not." This simple realization could be a crucial turning point in anyone's religious life, because it indicates an awareness of proportions. Human dignity rests on our efforts to be creative and intelligent, and yet it also requires a degree of realistic humility in the presence of the absolutely unknown and immeasurable.

In his novel *The Unnamable* Samuel Beckett says something equally paradoxical through his first-person character: "I who am here, who cannot speak, cannot think, and who must speak, and therefore perhaps think a little. . . ." How can we speak in the face of the vastness of the universe and conscious of the limitations of our language and our thinking? We can't speak, and yet we must. We can speak, as Beckett did, using words to evoke the hollowness and perimeters of our intelligence, words that express the paradox of not having the capacity and yet having the need to speak. The fifteenth-century theologian Nicolaus Cusanus is one among many mystics who say that we must cultivate our ignorance. "Mystical theology," which he sometimes equates with his idea of learned ignorance, he writes, in language that could come from Job or Beckett, "leads to freedom and silence . . . It's necessary to raise the mind above the meaning of words."

We have to find the appropriate attitude and language to speak the unspeakable and try to grasp the mystery that surrounds us. Modern-day churches and theologians seem to have trouble arriving at this point of theological sophistication, where language does not denote authoritatively but tentatively and poetically. Cusanus says we must use enigmatic images to evoke the mystery that is essentially unknowable. Beckett pursues the unnamable in language that tears apart all pretense of certainty, his novel deconstructing as it goes along.

The Book of Job, with its drama, poetry, and cast of characters, demonstrates in its very form the point of the story. Its power to move readers over generations is not explained by the precision with which it defines the relationship between humankind and the divine, but by the way it effectively goes beyond definition. It presses beyond the meaning of words to evoke the mystery, while clarifying the process by which we find a suitable posture in relation to the whirlwind. It is a lesson in intelligent ignorance. "I will lay my hand upon my mouth," says Job toward the end.

Why does an innocent, devoted person suffer? To make him stop talking, says The Book of Job, for there is no direct, easy answer to this most basic of questions. The proportions between the mystery and human capacity are so lopsided that the question has to be taken as a riddle. Its answer will be so far-fetched as to be laughable. We trust our intellect, analyses, methods, instruments, language, and encyclopedic reservoirs of knowledge too much. We have forgotten the ancient wisdom that speaks eloquently of silence and advises us to keep our words empty and our thoughts humble.

Job's life and possessions are restored to him after he discovers the virtue of silence. He and his friends have exhausted their words of complaint, explanation, and condemnation. Pointedly, the divine appears as a *voice* from a whirlwind, not a burning bush or a heavenly vision. This voice proclaims and celebrates its creativity and power in the world of nature, and its effect is simply to bring Job to respectful silence.

With respect to knowledge and expression, the religious life is not the same as the secular life. Each operates according to special principles and laws. Religion aspires to that level of consciousness where language trails off into silence, where emptiness is more impressive than substance, while secular research invents new words and new methods of thinking and always aims for substance. Sometimes religious institutions and religious people get confused and apply the rules of one to the other, saying too much about things that are best left mysterious. In that case, if we're lucky, we will hear a voice speaking from the whirlwind of our confusion.

The Book of Job describes religion as a path of silence, the route to a quiet place, beyond the realm of success and failure, where the voice of things can be heard and life can be restored. The resolution of Job's quandary takes place among the stars and the animals. These the Voice in the Whirlwind calls to mind. Why does an innocent man suffer? Because he is one with the innocent animals and the innocent stars. The riddle is not solved by human reason but by remembering the context of our lives. This memory stills all argument and blame, and ultimately restores life.

In the name of religion, for millennia people around the world have celebrated and praised the cycles of the stars and their seasons and the mysterious and beautiful expressive presence of animals. Religion has fused art and nature into rites that keep human life humane and ordered, rites that often echo the movements of the sky and use the images of animals to mimic the spirits. Without this kind of religion, we try to figure ourselves out and make a reasonable society. We make health or success our primary goals and money our bottom line. But the secular society fails, as we literalize the stars and allow animals to disappear from the planet.

Can we be silent again, recover the deep substance of religion, and restore our world? Maybe we need suffering to put us on the path to religion, to quiet our feverish secular activity. But how much will we have to suffer before we cry out, as Job did, finally perceiving the limitations of the human intellect and the possibility of our own self-destruction? History teaches us clearly that civilizations prosper and then die off or kill themselves with their own arrogance, but we seem not to take any lessons from this awareness.

In millions of books, films, tapes, and lectures we speak the speakable. Job had to learn to speak from his silence, to speak in a way that the quiet life was enhanced, and to use language in a way that evokes what is beyond language and conception. Religion and real art have known the secret of this kind of expression forever, but we have clearly entered an age where we think we can do without the childishness of ritual and the mysteries of art. It's difficult to imagine a time more in need of Job's riddling initiation than our own. Never before has humanity so needed to turn down the volume of its feverish productivity to hear the voice that reminds it of nature's sublimity and the foolish, humble foundations of its dignity and creativity.

The
BOOK
of JOB

CHAPTER ONE

There was a man in the land of Uz, whose name was Job; and that man was perfect and upright, and one that feared God, and eschewed evil.

2. And there were born unto him seven sons and three daughters.

3. His substance also was seven thousand sheep, and three thousand camels, and five hundred yoke of oxen, and five hundred she asses, and a very great household; so that this man was the greater of all the men of the east.

4. And his sons went and feasted in their houses, every one his day; and sent and called for their three sisters to eat and to drink with them.

5. And it was so, when the days of their feasting were gone about, that Job sent and sanctified them, and rose up early in the morning, and offered burnt offerings according to the number of them all: for Job said, It may be that my sons have sinned, and cursed God in their hearts. Thus did Job continually.

6. ¶Now there was a day when the sons of God came to present themselves before the LORD, and Satan came also among them.

7. And the LORD said unto Satan, Whence comest thou? Then Satan answered the LORD, and said, From going to and fro in the earth, and from walking up and down in it.

8. And the LORD said unto Satan, Hast thou considered my servant Job, that there is none like him in the earth, a perfect and an upright man, one that feareth God, and escheweth evil?

9. Then Satan answered the LORD, and said, Doth Job fear God for nought?

10. Hast not thou made an hedge about him, and about his house, and about all that he hath on every side? thou hast blessed the work of his hands, and his substance is increased in the land.

11. But put forth thine hand now, and touch all that he hath, and he will curse thee to thy face.

12. And the LORD said unto Satan, Behold, all that he hath is in thy power; only upon himself put not forth thine hand. So Satan went forth from the presence of the LORD.

13. ¶And there was a day when his sons and his daughters were eating and drinking wine in their eldest brother's house:

14. And there came a messenger unto Job, and said, The oxen were plowing, and the asses feeding beside them:

15. And the Sabeans fell upon them, and took them away; yea, they have slain the servants with the edge of the sword; and I only am escaped alone to tell thee.

16. While he was yet speaking, there came also another, and said, The fire of God is fallen from heaven, and hath burned up the sheep, and the servants, and consumed them; and I only am escaped alone to tell thee.

17. While he was yet speaking, there came also another, and said, The Chaldeans made out three bands, and fell upon the camels, and have carried them away, yea, and slain the servants with the edge of the sword; and I only am escaped alone to tell thee.

18. While he was yet speaking, there came also another, and said, Thy sons and thy daughters were eating and drinking wine in their eldest brother's house:

19. And, behold, there came a great wind from the wilderness, and smote the four corners of the house, and it fell upon the young men, and they are dead; and I only am escaped alone to tell thee.

20. Then Job arose, and rent his mantle, and shaved his head, and fell down upon the ground, and worshipped,

21. And said, Naked came I out of my mother's womb, and naked shall I return thither: the LORD gave, and the LORD hath taken away; blessed be the name of the LORD.

22. In all this Job sinned not, nor charged God foolishly.

CHAPTER TWO

Again there was a day when the sons of God came to present themselves before the LORD, and Satan came also among them to present himself before the LORD.

2. And the LORD said unto Satan; From whence comest thou? And Satan answered the LORD, and said, From going to and fro in the earth, and from walking up and down in it.

3. And the LORD said unto Satan, Hast thou considered my servant Job, that there is none like him in the earth, a perfect and an upright man, one that feareth God, and escheweth evil? and still he holdeth fast his integrity, although thou movedst me against him, to destroy him without cause.

4. And Satan answered the LORD, and said, Skin for skin, yea, all that a man hath will he give for his life.

5. But put forth thine hand now, and touch his bone and his flesh, and he will curse thee to thy face.

6. And the LORD said unto Satan, Behold, he is in thine hand; but save his life.

7. ¶So went Satan forth from the presence of the LORD, and smote Job with sore boils from the sole of his foot unto his crown.

8. And he took him a potsherd to scrape himself withal; and he sat down among the ashes.

9. ¶Then said his wife unto him, Dost thou still retain thine integrity? curse God, and die.

10. But he said unto her, Thou speakest as one of the foolish women speaketh. What? shall we receive good at the hand of God, and shall we not receive evil? In all this did not Job sin with his lips.

11. ¶Now when Job's three friends heard of all this evil that was come upon him, they came every one from his own place; Eliphaz the Temanite, and Bildad the Shuhite, and Zophar the Naamathite: for they had made an appointment together to come to mourn with him and to comfort him.

12. And when they lifted up their eyes afar off, and knew him not, they lifted up their voice, and wept; and they rent every one his mantle, and sprinkled dust upon their heads toward heaven.

13. So they sat down with him upon the ground seven days and seven nights, and none spake a word unto him; for they saw that his grief was very great.

CHAPTER THREE

After this opened Job his mouth, and cursed his day.

2. And Job spake, and said,

3. Let the day perish wherein I was born, and the night in which it was said, There is a man child conceived.

4. Let that day be darkness; let not God regard it from above, neither let the light shine upon it.

5. Let darkness and the shadow of death stain it; let a cloud dwell upon it; let the blackness of the day terrify it.

6. As for that night, let darkness seize upon it; let it not be joined unto the days of the year, let it not come into the number of the months.

7. Lo, let that night be solitary, let no joyful voice come therein.

8. Let them curse it that curse the day, who are ready to raise up their mourning.

9. Let the stars of the twilight thereof be dark; let it look for light, but have none; neither let it see the dawning of the day.

10. Because it shut not up the doors of my mother's womb, nor hid sorrow from mine eyes.

11. Why died I not from the womb? why did I not give up the ghost when I came out of the belly?

12. Why did the knees prevent me? or why the breasts that I should suck?

13. For now should I have lain still and been quiet, I should have slept: then had I been at rest,

14. With kings and counsellers of the earth, which built desolate places for themselves;

15. Or with princes that had gold, who filled their houses with silver:

16. Or as an hidden untimely birth I had not been; as infants which never saw light.

17. There the wicked cease from troubling; and there the weary be at rest.

18. There the prisoners rest together; they hear not the voice of the oppressor.

19. The small and great are there; and the servant is free from his master.

20. Wherefore is light given to him that is in misery, and life unto the bitter in soul;

21. Which long for death, but it cometh not; and dig for it more than for hid treasures;

22. Which rejoice exceedingly, and are glad, when they can find the grave?

23. Why is light given to a man whose way is hid, and whom God hath hedged in?

24. For my sighing cometh before I eat, and my roarings are poured out like the waters.

25. For the thing which I greatly feared is come upon me, and that which I was afraid of is come unto me.

26. I was not in safety, neither had I rest, neither was I quiet; yet trouble came.

CHAPTER FOUR

Then Elipnaz the Temanite answered and said,

2. If we assay to commune with thee, wilt thou be grieved? but who can withhold himself from speaking?

3. Behold, thou hast instructed many, and thou hast strengthened the weak hands.

4. Thy words have upholden him that was falling, and thou hast strengthened the feeble knees.

5. But now it is come upon thee, and thou faintest; it toucheth thee, and thou art troubled.

6. Is not this thy fear, thy confidence, thy hope, and the uprightness of thy ways?

7. Remember, I pray thee, who ever perished, being innocent? or where were the righteous cut off?

8. Even as I have seen, they that plow iniquity, and sow wickedness, reap the same.

9. By the blast of God they perish, and by the breath of his nostrils are they consumed.

10. The roaring of the lion, and the voice of the fierce lion, and the teeth of the young lions, are broken.

11. The old lion perisheth for lack of prey, and the stout lion's whelps are scattered abroad.

12. Now a thing was secretly brought to me, and mine ear received a little thereof.

13. In thoughts from the visions of the night, when deep sleep falleth on men,

14. Fear came upon me, and trembling, which made all my bones to shake.

15. Then a spirit passed before my face; the hair of my flesh stood up:

16. It stood still, but I could not discern the form thereof: an image was before mine eyes, there was silence, and I heard a voice, saying,

17. Shall mortal man be more just than God? shall a man be more pure than his maker?

18. Behold, he put no trust in his servants; and his angels he charged with folly:

19. How much less in them that dwell in houses of clay, whose foundation is in the dust, which are crushed before the moth?

20. They are destroyed from morning to evening: they perish for ever without any regarding it.

21. Doth not their excellency which is in them go away? they die, even without wisdom.

CHAPTER FIVE

Call now, if there be any that will answer thee; and to which of the saints wilt thou turn?

2. For wrath killeth the foolish man, and envy slayeth the silly one.

3. I have seen the foolish taking root: but suddenly I cursed his habitation.

4. His children are far from safety, and they are crushed in the gate, neither is there any to deliver them.

5. Whose harvest the hungry eateth up, and taketh it even out of the thorns, and the robber swalloweth up their substance.

6. Although affliction cometh not forth of the dust, neither doth trouble spring out of the ground;

7. Yet man is born unto trouble, as the sparks fly upward.

8. I would seek unto God, and unto God would I commit my cause:

9. Which doeth great things and unsearchable; marvellous things without number:

10. Who giveth rain upon the earth, and sendeth waters upon the fields:

11. To set up on high those that be low; that those which mourn may be exalted to safety.

12. He disappointeth the devices of the crafty, so that their hands cannot perform their enterprise.

13. He taketh the wise in their own craftiness: and the counsel of the froward is carried headlong.

14. They meet with darkness in the daytime, and grope in the noonday as in the night.

15. But he saveth the poor from the sword, from their mouth, and from the hand of the mighty.

16. So the poor hath hope, and iniquity stoppeth her mouth.

17. Behold, happy is the man whom God correcteth: therefore despise not thou the chastening of the Almighty:

18. For he maketh sore, and bindeth up: he woundeth, and his hands make whole.

19. He shall deliver thee in six troubles: yea, in seven there shall no evil touch thee.

20. In famine he shall redeem thee from death: and in war from the power of the sword.

21. Thou shalt be hid from the scourge of the tongue: neither shalt thou be afraid of destruction when it cometh.

22. At destruction and famine thou shalt laugh: neither shalt thou be afraid of the beasts of the earth.

23. For thou shalt be in league with the stones of the field: and the beasts of the field shall be at peace with thee.

24. And thou shalt know that thy tabernacle shall be in peace; and thou shalt visit thy habitation, and shalt not sin.

25. Thou shalt know also that thy seed shall be great, and thine offspring as the grass of the earth.

26. Thou shalt come to thy grave in a full age, like as a shock of corn cometh in in his season.

27. Lo this, we have searched it, so it is; hear it, and know thou it for thy good.

CHAPTER SIX

But Job answered and said,

2. Oh that my grief were throughly weighed, and my calamity laid in the balances together!

3. For now it would be heavier than the sand of the sea: therefore my words are swallowed up.

4. For the arrows of the Almighty are within me, the poison whereof drinketh up my spirit: the terrors of God do set themselves in array against me.

5. Doth the wild ass bray when he hath grass? or loweth the ox over his fodder?

6. Can that which is unsavoury be eaten without salt? or is there any taste in the white of an egg?

7. The things that my soul refused to touch are as my sorrowful meat.

8. Oh that I might have my request; and that God would grant me the thing that I long for!

9. Even that it would please God to destroy me; that he would let loose his hand, and cut me off!

10. Then should I yet have comfort; yea, I would harden myself in sorrow: let him not spare; for I have not concealed the words of the Holy One.

11. What is my strength, that I should hope? and what is mine end, that I should prolong my life?

12. Is my strength the strength of stones? or is my flesh of brass?

13. Is not my help in me? and is wisdom driven quite from me?

14. To him that is afflicted pity should be shewed from his friend; but he forsaketh the fear of the Almighty.

15. My brethren have dealt deceitfully as a brook, and as the stream of brooks they pass away;

16. Which are blackish by reason of the ice, and wherein the snow is hid:

17. What time they wax warm, they vanish: when it is hot, they are consumed out of their place.

18. The paths of their way are turned aside; they go to nothing, and perish.

19. The troops of Tema looked, the companies of Sheba waited for them.

20. They were confounded because they had hoped; they came thither, and were ashamed.

21. For now ye are nothing; ye see my casting down, and are afraid.

22. Did I say, Bring unto me? or, Give a reward for me of your substance?

23. Or, Deliver me from the enemy's hand? or, Redeem me from the hand of the mighty?

24. Teach me, and I will hold my tongue: and cause me to understand wherein I have erred.

25. How forcible are right words! but what doth your arguing reprove?

26. Do ye imagine to reprove words, and the speeches of one that is desperate, which are as wind?

27. Yea, ye overwhelm the fatherless, and ye dig a pit for your friend.

28. Now therefore be content, look upon me; for it is evident unto you if I lie.

29. Return, I pray you, let it not be iniquity; yea, return again, my righteousness is in it.

30. Is there iniquity in my tongue? cannot my taste discern perverse things?

CHAPTER SEVEN

Is there not an appointed time to man upon earth? are not his days also like the days of an hireling?

2. As a servant earnestly desireth the shadow, and as an hireling looketh for the reward of his work:

3. So am I made to possess months of vanity, and wearisome nights are appointed to me.

4. When I lie down, I say, When shall I arise, and the night be gone? and I am full of tossings to and fro unto the dawning of the day.

5. My flesh is clothed with worms and clods of dust; my skin is broken, and become loathsome.

6. My days are swifter than a weaver's shuttle, and are spent without hope.

7. O remember that my life is wind: mine eye shall no more see good.

8. The eye of him that hath seen me shall see me no more: thine eyes are upon me, and I am not.

9. As the cloud is consumed and vanisheth away: so he that goeth down to the grave shall come up no more.

10. He shall return no more to his house, neither shall his place know him any more.

11. Therefore I will not refrain my mouth; I will speak in the anguish of my spirit; I will complain in the bitterness of my soul.

12. Am I a sea, or a whale, that thou settest a watch over me?

13. When I say, My bed shall comfort me, my couch shall ease my complaint;

14. Then thou scarest me with dreams, and terrifiest me through visions:

15. So that my soul chooseth strangling, and death rather than my life.

16. I loathe it; I would not live always: let me alone; for my days are vanity.

17. What is man, that thou shouldest magnify him? and that thou shouldest set thine heart upon him?

18. And that thou shouldest visit him every morning, and try him every moment?

19. How long wilt thou not depart from me, nor let me alone till I swallow down my spittle?

20. I have sinned; what shall I do unto thee, O thou preserver of men? why hast thou set me as a mark against thee, so that I am a burden to myself?

21. And why dost thou not pardon my transgression, and take away mine iniquity? for now shall I sleep in the dust; and thou shalt seek me in the morning, but I shall not be.

CHAPTER EIGHT

Then answered Bildad the Shuhite, and said,

2. How long wilt thou speak these things? and how long shall the words of thy mouth be like a strong wind?

3. Doth God pervert judgment? or doth the Almighty pervert justice?

4. If thy children have sinned against him; and he have cast them away for their transgression;

5. If thou wouldest seek unto God betimes, and make thy supplication to the Almighty;

6. If thou wert pure and upright; surely now he would awake for thee, and make the habitation of thy righteousness prosperous.

7. Though thy beginning was small, yet thy latter end should greatly increase.

8. For inquire, I pray thee, of the former age, and prepare thyself to the search of their fathers:

9. (For we are but of yesterday, and know nothing, because our days upon earth are a shadow:)

10. Shall not they teach thee, and tell thee, and utter words out of their heart?

11. Can the rush grow up without mire? can the flag grow without water?

12. Whilst it is yet in his greenness, and not cut down, it withereth before any other herb.

13. So are the paths of all that forget God; and the hypocrite's hope shall perish:

14. Whose hope shall be cut off, and whose trust shall be a spider's web.

15. He shall lean upon his house, but it shall not stand: he shall hold it fast, but it shall not endure.

16. He is green before the sun, and his branch shooteth forth in his garden.

17. His roots are wrapped about the heap, and seeth the place of stones.

18. If he destroy him from his place, then it shall deny him, saying, I have not seen thee.

19. Behold, this is the joy of his way, and out of the earth shall others grow.

20. Behold, God will not cast away a perfect man, neither will he help the evil doers:

21. Till he fill thy mouth with laughing, and thy lips with rejoicing.

22. They that hate thee shall be clothed with shame; and the dwelling place of the wicked shall come to nought.

CHAPTER NINE

Then Job answered and said,

2. I know it is so of a truth: but how should man be just with God?

3. If he will contend with him, he cannot answer him one of a thousand.

4. He is wise in heart, and mighty in strength: who hath hardened himself against him, and hath prospered?

5. Which removeth the mountains, and they know not: which overturneth them in his anger.

6. Which shaketh the earth out of her place, and the pillars thereof tremble.

7. Which commandeth the sun, and it riseth not; and sealeth up the stars.

8. Which alone spreadeth out the heavens, and treadeth upon the waves of the sea.

9. Which maketh Arcturus, Orion, and Pleiades, and the chambers of the south.

10. Which doeth great things past finding out; yea, and wonders without number.

11. Lo, he goeth by me, and I see him not: he passeth on also, but I perceive him not.

12. Behold, he taketh away, who can hinder him? who will say unto him, What doest thou?

13. If God will not withdraw his anger, the proud helpers do stoop under him.

14. How much less shall I answer him, and choose out my words to reason with him?

15. Whom, though I were righteous, yet would I not answer, but I would make supplication to my judge.

16. If I had called, and he had answered me; yet would I not believe that he had hearkened unto my voice.

17. For he breaketh me with a tempest, and multiplieth my wounds without cause.

18. He will not suffer me to take my breath, but filleth me with bitterness.

19. If I speak of strength, lo, he is strong: and if of judgment, who shall set me a time to plead?

20. If I justify myself, mine own mouth shall condemn me: if I say, I am perfect, it shall also prove me perverse.

21. Though I were perfect, yet would I not know my soul: I would despise my life.

22. This is one thing, therefore I said it, He destroyeth the perfect and the wicked.

23. If the scourge slay suddenly, he will laugh at the trial of the innocent.

24. The earth is given into the hand of the wicked: he covereth the faces of the judges thereof; if not, where, and who is he?

25. Now my days are swifter than a post: they flee away, they see no good.

26. They are passed away as the swift ships: as the eagle that hasteth to the prey.

27. If I say, I will forget my complaint, I will leave off my heaviness, and comfort myself:

28. I am afraid of all my sorrows, I know that thou wilt not hold me innocent.

29. If I be wicked, why then labour I in vain?

30. If I wash myself with snow water, and make my hands never so clean;

31. Yet shalt thou plunge me in the ditch, and mine own clothes shall abhor me.

32. For he is not a man, as I am, that I should answer him, and we should come together in judgment.

33. Neither is there any daysman betwixt us, that might lay his hand upon us both.

34. Let him take his rod away from me, and let not his fear terrify me:

35. Then would I speak, and not fear him; but it is not so with me.

CHAPTER TEN

My soul is weary of my life; I will leave my complaint upon myself; I will speak in the bitterness of my soul.

2. I will say unto God, Do not condemn me; shew me wherefore thou contendest with me.

3. Is it good unto thee that thou shouldest oppress, that thou shouldest despise the work of thine hands, and shine upon the counsel of the wicked?

4. Hast thou eyes of flesh? or seest thou as man seeth?

5. Are thy days as the days of man? are thy years as man's days,

6. That thou inquirest after mine iniquity, and searchest after my sin?

7. Thou knowest that I am not wicked; and there is none that can deliver out of thine hand.

8. Thine hands have made me and fashioned me together round about; yet thou dost destroy me.

9. Remember, I beseech thee, that thou hast made me as the clay; and wilt thou bring me into dust again?

10. Hast thou not poured me out as milk, and curdled me like cheese?

11. Thou hast clothed me with skin and flesh, and hast fenced me with bones and sinews.

12. Thou hast granted me life and favour, and thy visitation hath preserved my spirit.

13. And these things hast thou hid in thine heart: I know that this is with thee.

14. If I sin, then thou markest me, and thou wilt not acquit me from mine iniquity.

15. If I be wicked, woe unto me; and if I be righteous, yet will I not lift up my head. I am full of confusion; therefore see thou mine affliction;

16. For it increaseth. Thou huntest me as a fierce lion: and again thou shewest thyself marvellous upon me.

17. Thou renewest thy witnesses against me, and increasest thine indignation upon me; changes and war are against me.

18. Wherefore then hast thou brought me forth out of the womb? Oh that I had given up the ghost, and no eye had seen me!

19. I should have been as though I had not been; I should have been carried from the womb to the grave.

20. Are not my days few? cease then, and let me alone, that I may take comfort a little,

21. Before I go whence I shall not return, even to the land of darkness and the shadow of death;

22. A land of darkness, as darkness itself; and of the shadow of death, without any order, and where the light is as darkness.

CHAPTER ELEVEN

Then answered Zophar the Naamathite, and said,

2. Should not the multitude of words be answered? and should a man full of talk be justified?

3. Should thy lies make men hold their peace? and when thou mockest, shall no man make thee ashamed?

4. For thou hast said, My doctrine is pure, and I am clean in thine eyes.

5. But oh that God would speak, and open his lips against thee;

6. And that he would shew thee the secrets of wisdom, that they are double to that which is! Know therefore that God exacteth of thee less than thine iniquity deserveth.

7. Canst thou by searching find out God? canst thou find out the Almighty unto perfection?

8. It is as high as heaven; what canst thou do? deeper than hell; what canst thou know?

9. The measure thereof is longer than the earth, and broader than the sea.

10. If he cut off, and shut up, or gather together, then who can hinder him?

11. For he knoweth vain men: he seeth wickedness also; will he not then consider it?

12. For vain man would be wise, though man be born like a wild ass's colt.

13. If thou prepare thine heart, and stretch out thine hands toward him;

14. If iniquity be in thine hand, put it far away, and let not wickedness dwell in thy tabernacles.

15. For then shalt thou lift up thy face without spot; yea, thou shalt be stedfast, and shalt not fear:

16. Because thou shalt forget thy misery, and remember it as waters that pass away:

17. And thine age shall be clearer than the noonday; thou shalt shine forth, thou shalt be as the morning.

18. And thou shalt be secure, because there is hope; yea, thou shalt dig about thee, and thou shalt take thy rest in safety.

19. Also thou shalt lie down, and none shall make thee afraid; yea, many shall make suit unto thee.

20. But the eyes of the wicked shall fail, and they shall not escape, and their hope shall be as the giving up of the ghost.

CHAPTER TWELVE

And Job answered and said,

2. No doubt but ye are the people, and wisdom shall die with you.

3. But I have understanding as well as you; I am not inferior to you: yea, who knoweth not such things as these?

4. I am as one mocked of his neighbour, who calleth upon God, and he answereth him: the just upright man is laughed to scorn.

5. He that is ready to slip with his feet is as a lamp despised in the thought of him that is at ease.

6. The tabernacles of robbers prosper, and they that provoke God are secure; into whose hand God bringeth abundantly.

7. But ask now the beasts, and they shall teach thee; and the fowls of the air, and they shall tell thee:

8. Or speak to the earth, and it shall teach thee: and the fishes of the sea shall declare unto thee.

9. Who knoweth not in all these that the hand of the LORD hath wrought this?

10. In whose hand is the soul of every living thing, and the breath of all mankind.

11. Doth not the ear try words? and the mouth taste his meat?

12. With the ancient is wisdom; and in length of days understanding.

13. With him is wisdom and strength, he hath counsel and understanding.

14. Behold, he breaketh down, and it cannot be built again: he shutteth up a man, and there can be no opening.

15. Behold, he withholdeth the waters, and they dry up: also he sendeth them out, and they overturn the earth.

16. With him is strength and wisdom: the deceived and the deceiver are his.

17. He leadeth counsellers away spoiled, and maketh the judges fools.

18. He looseth the bond of kings, and girdeth their loins with a girdle.

19. He leadeth princes away spoiled, and overthroweth the mighty.

20. He removeth away the speech of the trusty, and taketh away the understanding of the aged.

21. He poureth contempt upon princes, and weakeneth the strength of the mighty.

22. He discovereth deep things out of darkness, and bringeth out to light the shadow of death.

23. He increaseth the nations, and destroyeth them: he enlargeth the nations, and straiteneth them again.

24. He taketh away the heart of the chief of the people of the earth, and causeth them to wander in a wilderness where there is no way.

25. They grope in the dark without light, and he maketh them to stagger like a drunken man.

CHAPTER THIRTEEN

Lo, mine eye hath seen all this, mine ear hath heard and understood it.

2. What ye know, the same do I know also: I am not inferior unto you.

3. Surely I would speak to the Almighty, and I desire to reason with God.

4. But ye are forgers of lies, ye are all physicians of no value.

5. O that ye would altogether hold your peace! and it should be your wisdom.

6. Hear now my reasoning, and hearken to the pleadings of my lips.

7. Will ye speak wickedly for God? and talk deceitfully for him?

8. Will ye accept his person? will ye contend for God?

9. Is it good that he should search you out? or as one man mocketh another, do ye so mock him?

10. He will surely reprove you, if ye do secretly acccpt persons.

11. Shall not his excellency make you afraid? and his dread fall upon you?

12. Your remembrances are like unto ashes, your bodies to bodies of clay.

13. Hold your peace, let me alone, that I may speak, and let come on me what will.

14. Wherefore do I take my flesh in my teeth, and put my life in mine hand?

15. Though he slay me, yet will I trust in him: but I will maintain mine own ways before him.

16. He also shall be my salvation: for an hypocrite shall not come before him.

17. Hear diligently my speech, and my declaration with your ears.

18. Behold now, I have ordered my cause; I know that I shall be justified.

19. Who is he that will plead with me? for now, if I hold my tongue, I shall give up the ghost.

20. Only do not two things unto me: then will I not hide myself from thee.

21. Withdraw thine hand far from me: and let not thy dread make me afraid.

22. Then call thou, and I will answer: or let me speak, and answer thou me.

23. How many are mine iniquities and sins? make me to know my transgression and my sin.

24. Wherefore hidest thou thy face, and holdest me for thine enemy?

25. Wilt thou break a leaf driven to and fro? and wilt thou pursue the dry stubble?

26. For thou writest bitter things against me, and makest me to possess the iniquities of my youth.

27. Thou puttest my feet also in the stocks, and lookest narrowly unto all my paths; thou settest a print upon the heels of my feet.

28. And he, as a rotten thing, consumeth, as a garment that is moth eaten.

CHAPTER FOURTEEN

Man that is born of a woman is of few days, and full of trouble.

2. He cometh forth like a flower, and is cut down: he fleeth also as a shadow, and continueth not.

3. And dost thou open thine eyes upon such a one, and bringest me into judgment with thee?

4. Who can bring a clean thing out of an unclean? not one.

5. Seeing his days are determined, the number of his months are with thee, thou hast appointed his bounds that he cannot pass;

6. Turn from him, that he may rest, till he shall accomplish, as an hireling, his day.

7. For there is hope of a tree, if it be cut down, that it will sprout again, and that the tender branch thereof will not cease.

8. Though the root thereof wax old in the earth, and the stock thereof die in the ground;

9. Yet through the scent of water it will bud, and bring forth boughs like a plant.

10. But man dieth, and wasteth away: yea, man giveth up the ghost, and where is he?

11. As the waters fail from the sea, and the flood decayeth and drieth up:

12. So man lieth down, and riseth not: till the heavens be no more, they shall not awake, nor be raised out of their sleep.

13. O that thou wouldest hide me in the grave, that thou wouldest keep me secret, until thy wrath be past, that thou wouldest appoint me a set time, and remember me!

14. If a man die, shall he live again? all the days of my appointed time will I wait, till my change come.

15. Thou shalt call, and I will answer thee: thou wilt have a desire to the work of thine hands.

16. For now thou numberest my steps: dost thou not watch over my sin?

17. My transgression is sealed up in a bag, and thou sewest up mine iniquity.

18. And surely the mountain falling cometh to nought, and the rock is removed out of his place.

19. The waters wear the stones: thou washest away the things which grow out of the dust of the earth; and thou destroyest the hope of man.

20. Thou prevailest for ever against him, and he passeth: thou changest his countenance, and sendest him away.

21. His sons come to honour, and he knoweth it not; and they are brought low, but he perceiveth it not of them.

22. But his flesh upon him shall have pain, and his soul within him shall mourn.

CHAPTER FIFTEEN

Then answered Eliphaz the Temanite, and said,

2. Should a wise man utter vain knowledge, and fill his belly with the east wind?

3. Should he reason with unprofitable talk? or with speeches wherewith he can do no good?

4. Yea, thou castest off fear, and restrainest prayer before God.

5. For thy mouth uttereth thine iniquity, and thou choosest the tongue of the crafty.

6. Thine own mouth condemneth thee, and not I: yea, thine own lips testify against thee.

7. Art thou the first man that was born? or wast thou made before the hills?

8. Hast thou heard the secret of God? and dost thou restrain wisdom to thyself?

9. What knowest thou, that we know not? what understandest thou, which is not in us?

10. With us are both the grayheaded and very aged men, much elder than thy father.

11. Are the consolations of God small with thee? is there any secret thing with thee?

12. Why doth thine heart carry thee away? and what do thy eyes wink at,

13. That thou turnest thy spirit against God, and lettest such words go out of thy mouth?

14. What is man, that he should be clean? and he which is born of a woman, that he should be righteous?

15. Behold, he putteth no trust in his saints; yea, the heavens are not clean in his sight.

16. How much more abominable and filthy is man, which drinketh iniquity like water?

17. I will shew thee, hear me; and that which I have seen I will declare;

18. Which wise men have told from their fathers, and have not hid it:

19. Unto whom alone the earth was given, and no stranger passed among them.

20. The wicked man travaileth with pain all his days, and the number of years is hidden to the oppressor.

21. A dreadful sound is in his ears: in prosperity the destroyer shall come upon him.

22. He believeth not that he shall return out of darkness, and he is waited for of the sword.

23. He wandereth abroad for bread, saying, Where is it? he knoweth that the day of darkness is ready at his hand.

24. Trouble and anguish shall make him afraid, they shall prevail against him, as a king ready to the battle.

25. For he stretcheth out his hand against God, and strengtheneth himself against the Almighty.

26. He runneth upon him, even on his neck, upon the thick bosses of his bucklers:

27. Because he covereth his face with his fatness, and maketh collops of fat on his flanks.

28. And he dwelleth in desolate cities, and in houses which no man inhabiteth, which are ready to become heaps.

29. He shall not be rich, neither shall his substance continue, neither shall he prolong the perfection thereof upon the earth.

30. He shall not depart out of darkness; the flame shall dry up his branches, and by the breath of his mouth shall he go away.

31. Let not him that is deceived trust in vanity: for vanity shall be his recompence.

32. It shall be accomplished before his time, and his branch shall not be green.

33. He shall shake off his unripe grape as the vine, and shall cast off his flower as the olive.

34. For the congregation of hypocrites shall be desolate, and fire shall consume the tabernacles of bribery.

35. They conceive mischief, and bring forth vanity, and their belly prepareth deceit.

Chapter Sixteen

Then Job answered and said,

2. I have heard many such things: miserable comforters are ye all.

3. Shall vain words have an end? or what emboldeneth thee that thou answerest?

4. I also could speak as ye do: if your soul were in my soul's stead, I could heap up words against you, and shake mine head at you.

5. But I would strengthen you with my mouth, and the moving of my lips should asswage your grief.

6. Though I speak, my grief is not asswaged: and though I forbear, what am I eased?

7. But now he hath made me weary: thou hast made desolate all my company.

8. And thou hast filled me with wrinkles, which is a witness against me: and my leanness rising up in me beareth witness to my face.

9. He teareth me in his wrath, who hateth me: he gnasheth upon me with his teeth; mine enemy sharpeneth his eyes upon me.

10. They have gaped upon me with their mouth; they have smitten me upon the cheek reproachfully; they have gathered themselves together against me.

11. God hath delivered me to the ungodly, and turned me over into the hands of the wicked.

12. I was at ease, but he hath broken me asunder: he hath also taken me by my neck, and shaken me to pieces, and set me up for his mark.

13. His archers compass me round about, he cleaveth my reins asunder, and doth not spare; he poureth out my gall upon the ground.

14. He breaketh me with breach upon breach, he runneth upon me like a giant.

15. I have sewed sackcloth upon my skin, and defiled my horn in the dust.

16. My face is foul with weeping, and on my eyelids is the shadow of death;

17. Not for any injustice in mine hands: also my prayer is pure.

18. O earth, cover not thou my blood, and let my cry have no place.

19. Also now, behold, my witness is in heaven, and my record is on high.

20. My friends scorn me: but mine eye poureth out tears unto God.

21. O that one might plead for a man with God, as a man pleadeth for his neighbour!

22. When a few years are come, then I shall go the way whence I shall not return.

CHAPTER SEVENTEEN

My breath is corrupt, my days are extinct, the graves are ready for me.

2. Are there not mockers with me? and doth not mine eye continue in their provocation?

3. Lay down now, put me in a surety with thee; who is he that will strike hands with me?

4. For thou hast hid their heart from understanding: therefore shalt thou not exalt them.

5. He that speaketh flattery to his friends, even the eyes of his children shall fail.

6. He hath made me also a byword of the people; and aforetime I was as a tabret.

7. Mine eye also is dim by reason of sorrow, and all my members are as a shadow.

8. Upright men shall be astonied at this, and the innocent shall stir up himself against the hypocrite.

9. The righteous also shall hold on his way, and he that hath clean hands shall be stronger and stronger.

10. But as for you all, do ye return, and come now: for I cannot find one wise man among you.

11. My days are past, my purposes are broken off, even the thoughts of my heart.

12. They change the night into day: the light is short because of darkness.

13. If I wait, the grave is mine house: I have made my bed in the darkness.

14. I have said to corruption, Thou art my father: to the worm, Thou art my mother, and my sister.

15. And where is now my hope? as for my hope, who shall see it?

16. They shall go down to the bars of the pit, when our rest together is in the dust.

CHAPTER EIGHTEEN

Then answered Bildad the Shuhite, and said,

2. How long will it be ere ye make an end of words? mark, and afterwards we will speak.

3. Wherefore are we counted as beasts, and reputed vile in your sight?

4. He teareth himself in his anger: shall the earth be forsaken for thee? and shall the rock be removed out of his place?

5. Yea, the light of the wicked shall be put out, and the spark of his fire shall not shine.

6. The light shall be dark in his tabernacle, and his candle shall be put out with him.

7. The steps of his strength shall be straitened, and his own counsel shall cast him down.

8. For he is cast into a net by his own feet, and he walketh upon a snare.

9. The gin shall take him by the heel, and the robber shall prevail against him.

10. The snare is laid for him in the ground, and a trap for him in the way.

11. Terrors shall make him afraid on every side, and shall drive him to his feet.

12. His strength shall be hungerbitten, and destruction shall be ready at his side.

13. It shall devour the strength of his skin: even the firstborn of death shall devour his strength.

14. His confidence shall be rooted out of his tabernacle, and it shall bring him to the king of terrors.

15. It shall dwell in his tabernacle, because it is none of his: brimstone shall be scattered upon his habitation.

16. His roots shall be dried up beneath, and above shall his branch be cut off.

17. His remembrance shall perish from the earth, and he shall have no name in the street.

18. He shall be driven from light into darkness, and chased out of the world.

19. He shall neither have son nor nephew among his people, nor any remaining in his dwellings.

20. They that come after him shall be astonied at his day, as they that went before were affrighted.

21. Surely such are the dwellings of the wicked, and this is the place of him that knoweth not God.

CHAPTER NINETEEN

Then Job answered and said,

2. How long will ye vex my soul, and break me in pieces with words?

3. These ten times have ye reproached me: ye are not ashamed that ye make yourselves strange to me.

4. And be it indeed that I have erred, mine error remaineth with myself.

5. If indeed ye will magnify yourselves against me, and plead against me my reproach:

6. Know now that God hath overthrown me, and hath compassed me with his net.

7. Behold, I cry out of wrong, but I am not heard: I cry aloud, but there is no judgment.

8. He hath fenced up my way that I cannot pass, and he hath set darkness in my paths.

9. He hath stripped me of my glory, and taken the crown from my head.

10. He hath destroyed me on every side, and I am gone: and mine hope hath he removed like a tree.

11. He hath also kindled his wrath against me, and he counteth me unto him as one of his enemies.

12. His troops come together, and raise up their way against me, and encamp round about my tabernacle.

13. He hath put my brethren far from me, and mine acquaintance are verily estranged from me.

14. My kinsfolk have failed, and my familiar friends have forgotten me.

15. They that dwell in mine house, and my maids, count me for a stranger: I am an alien in their sight.

16. I called my servant, and he gave me no answer; I intreated him with my mouth.

17. My breath is strange to my wife, though I intreated for the children's sake of mine own body.

18. Yea, young children despised me; I arose, and they spake against me.

19. All my inward friends abhorred me: and they whom I loved are turned against me.

20. My bone cleaveth to my skin and to my flesh, and I am escaped with the skin of my teeth.

21. Have pity upon me, have pity upon me, O ye my friends; for the hand of God hath touched me.

22. Why do ye persecute me as God, and are not satisfied with my flesh?

23. Oh that my words were now written! oh that they were printed in a book!

24. That they were graven with an iron pen and lead in the rock for ever!

25. For I know that my redeemer liveth, and that he shall stand at the latter day upon the earth:

26. And though after my skin worms destroy this body, yet in my flesh shall I see God:

27. Whom I shall see for myself, and mine eyes shall behold, and not another; though my reins be consumed within me.

28. But ye should say, Why persecute we him, seeing the root of the matter is found in me?

29. Be ye afraid of the sword: for wrath bringeth the punishments of the sword, that ye may know there is a judgment.

Chapter Twenty

Then answered Zophar the Naamathite, and said,

2. Therefore do my thoughts cause me to answer, and for this I make haste.

3. I have heard the check of my reproach, and the spirit of my understanding causeth me to answer.

4. Knowest thou not this of old, since man was placed upon earth,

5. That the triumphing of the wicked is short, and the joy of the hypocrite but for a moment?

6. Though his excellency mount up to the heavens, and his head reach unto the clouds;

7. Yet he shall perish for ever like his own dung: they which have seen him shall say, Where is he?

8. He shall fly away as a dream, and shall not be found: yea, he shall be chased away as a vision of the night.

9. The eye also which saw him shall see him no more; neither shall his place any more behold him.

10. His children shall seek to please the poor, and his hands shall restore their goods.

11. His bones are full of the sin of his youth, which shall lie down with him in the dust.

12. Though wickedness be sweet in his mouth, though he hide it under his tongue;

13. Though he spare it, and forsake it not; but keep it still within his mouth:

14. Yet his meat in his bowels is turned, it is the gall of asps within him.

15. He hath swallowed down riches, and he shall vomit them up again: God shall cast them out of his belly.

16. He shall suck the poison of asps: the viper's tongue shall slay him.

17. He shall not see the rivers, the floods, the brooks of honey and butter.

18. That which he laboured for shall he restore, and shall not swallow it down: according to his substance shall the restitution be, and he shall not rejoice therein.

19. Because he hath oppressed and hath forsaken the poor; because he hath violently taken away an house which he builded not;

20. Surely he shall not feel quietness in his belly, he shall not save of that which he desired.

21. There shall none of his meat be left; therefore shall no man look for his goods.

22. In the fulness of his sufficiency he shall be in straits: every hand of the wicked shall come upon him.

23. When he is about to fill his belly, God shall cast the fury of his wrath upon him, and shall rain it upon him while he is eating.

24. He shall flee from the iron weapon and the bow of steel shall strike him through.

25. It is drawn, and cometh out of the body; yea, the glittering sword cometh out of his gall: terrors are upon him.

26. All darkness shall be hid in his secret places: a fire not blown shall consume him; it shall go ill with him that is left in his tabernacle.

27. The heaven shall reveal his iniquity; and the earth shall rise up against him.

28. The increase of his house shall depart, and his goods shall flow away in the day of his wrath.

29. This is the portion of a wicked man from God, and the heritage appointed unto him by God.

CHAPTER TWENTY-ONE

But Job answered and said,

2. Hear diligently my speech, and let this be your consolations.

3. Suffer me that I may speak; and after that I have spoken, mock on.

4. As for me, is my complaint to man? and if it were so, why should not my spirit be troubled?

5. Mark me, and be astonished, and lay your hand upon your mouth.

6. Even when I remember I am afraid, and trembling taketh hold on my flesh.

7. Wherefore do the wicked live, become old, yea, are mighty in power?

8. Their seed is established in their sight with them, and their offspring before their eyes.

9. Their houses are safe from fear, neither is the rod of God upon them.

10. Their bull gendereth, and faileth not; their cow calveth, and casteth not her calf.

11. They send forth their little ones like a flock, and their children dance.

12. They take the timbrel and harp, and rejoice at the sound of the organ.

13. They spend their days in wealth, and in a moment go down to the grave.

14. Therefore they say unto God, Depart from us; for we desire not the knowledge of thy ways.

15. What is the Almighty, that we should serve him? and what profit should we have, if we pray unto him?

16. Lo, their good is not in their hand: the counsel of the wicked is far from me.

17. How oft is the candle of the wicked put out! and how oft cometh their destruction upon them! God distributeth sorrows in his anger.

18. They are as stubble before the wind, and as chaff that the storm carrieth away.

19. God layeth up his iniquity for his children: he rewardeth him, and he shall know it.

20. His eyes shall see his destruction, and he shall drink of the wrath of the Almighty.

21. For what pleasure hath he in his house after him, when the number of his months is cut off in the midst?

22. Shall any teach God knowledge? seeing he judgeth those that are high.

23. One dieth in his full strength, being wholly at ease and quiet.

24. His breasts are full of milk, and his bones are moistened with marrow.

25. And another dieth in the bitterness of his soul, and never eateth with pleasure.

26. They shall lie down alike in the dust, and the worms shall cover them.

27. Behold, I know your thoughts, and the devices which ye wrongfully imagine against me.

28. For ye say, Where is the house of the prince? and where are the dwelling places of the wicked?

29. Have ye not asked them that go by the way? and do ye not know their tokens,

30. That the wicked is reserved to the day of destruction? they shall be brought forth to the day of wrath.

31. Who shall declare his way to his face? and who shall repay him what he hath done?

32. Yet shall he be brought to the grave, and shall remain in the tomb.

33. The clods of the valley shall be sweet unto him, and every man shall draw after him, as there are innumerable before him.

34. How then comfort ye me in vain, seeing in your answers there remaineth falsehood?

CHAPTER TWENTY-TWO

Then Eliphaz the Temanite answered and said,

2. Can a man be profitable unto God, as he that is wise may be profitable unto himself?

3. Is it any pleasure to the Almighty, that thou art righteous? or is it gain to him, that thou makest thy ways perfect?

4. Will he reprove thee for fear of thee? will he enter with thee into judgment?

5. Is not thy wickedness great? and thine iniquities infinite?

6. For thou hast taken a pledge from thy brother for nought, and stripped the naked of their clothing.

7. Thou hast not given water to the weary to drink, and thou hast withholden bread from the hungry.

8. But as for the mighty man, he had the earth; and the honourable man dwelt in it.

9. Thou hast sent widows away empty, and the arms of the fatherless have been broken.

10. Therefore snares are round about thee, and sudden fear troubleth thee;

11. Or darkness, that thou canst not see; and abundance of waters cover thee.

12. Is not God in the height of heaven? and behold the height of the stars, how high they are!

13. And thou sayest, How doth God know? can he judge through the dark cloud?

14. Thick clouds are a covering to him, that he seeth not; and he walketh in the circuit of heaven.

15. Hast thou marked the old way which wicked men have trodden?

16. Which were cut down out of time, whose foundation was overflown with a flood:

17. Which said unto God, Depart from us: and what can the Almighty do for them?

18. Yet he filled their houses with good things: but the counsel of the wicked is far from me.

19. The righteous see it, and are glad: and the innocent laugh them to scorn.

20. Whereas our substance is not cut down, but the remnant of them the fire consumeth.

21. Acquaint now thyself with him, and be at peace: thereby good shall come unto thee.

22. Receive, I pray thee, the law from his mouth, and lay up his words in thine heart.

23. If thou return to the Almighty, thou shalt be built up, thou shalt put away iniquity far from thy tabernacles.

24. Then shalt thou lay up gold as dust, and the gold of Ophir as the stones of the brooks.

25. Yea, the Almighty shall be thy defence, and thou shalt have plenty of silver.

26. For then shalt thou have they delight in the Almighty, and shalt lift up thy face unto God.

27. Thou shalt make thy prayer unto him, and he shall hear thee, and thou shalt pay thy vows.

28. Thou shalt also decree a thing, and it shall be established unto thee: and the light shall shine upon thy ways.

29. When men are cast down, then thou shalt say, There is lifting up; and he shall save the humble person.

30. He shall deliver the island of the innocent: and it is delivered by the pureness of thine hands.

CHAPTER TWENTY-THREE

Then Job answered and said,

2. Even to day is my complaint bitter: my stroke is heavier than my groaning.

3. Oh that I knew where I might find him! that I might come even to his seat!

4. I would order my cause before him, and fill my mouth with arguments.

5. I would know the words which he would answer me, and understand what he would say unto me.

6. Will he plead against me with his great power? No; but he would put strength in me.

7. There the righteous might dispute with him; so should I be delivered for ever from my judge.

8. Behold, I go forward, but he is not there; and backward, but I cannot perceive him:

9. On the left hand, where he doth work, but I cannot behold him: he hideth himself on the right hand, that I cannot see him:

10. But he knoweth the way that I take: when he hath tried me, I shall come forth as gold.

11. My foot hath held his steps, his way have I kept, and not declined.

12. Neither have I gone back from the commandment of his lips; I have esteemed the words of his mouth more than my necessary food.

13. But he is in one mind, and who can turn him? and what his soul desireth, even that he doeth.

14. For he performeth the thing that is appointed for me: and many such things are with him.

15. Therefore am I troubled at his presence: when I consider, I am afraid of him.

16. For God maketh my heart soft, and the Almighty troubleth me:

17. Because I was not cut off before the darkness, neither hath he covered the darkness from my face.

CHAPTER TWENTY-FOUR

Why, seeing times are not hidden from the Almighty, do they that know him not see his days?

2. Some remove the landmarks; they violently take away flocks, and feed thereof.

3. They drive away the ass of the fatherless, they take the widow's ox for a pledge.

4. They turn the needy out of the way: the poor of the earth hide themselves together.

5. Behold, as wild asses in the desert, go they forth to their work; rising betimes for a prey: the wilderness yieldeth food for them and for their children.

6. They reap every one his corn in the field: and they gather the vintage of the wicked.

7. They cause the naked to lodge without clothing, that they have no covering in the cold.

8. They are wet with the showers of the mountains, and embrace the rock for want of a shelter.

9. They pluck the fatherless from the breast, and take a pledge of the poor.

10. They cause him to go naked without clothing, and they take away the sheaf from the hungry;

11. Which make oil within their walls, and tread their wine-presses, and suffer thirst.

12. Men groan from out of the city, and the soul of the wounded crieth out: yet God layeth not folly to them.

13. They are of those that rebel against the light; they know not the ways thereof, nor abide in the paths thereof.

14. The murderer rising with the light killeth the poor and needy, and in the night is as a thief.

15. The eye also of the adulterer waiteth for the twilight, saying, No eye shall see me: and disguiseth his face.

16. In the dark they dig through houses, which they had marked for themselves in the daytime: they know not the light.

17. For the morning is to them even as the shadow of death: if one know them, they are in the terrors of the shadow of death.

18. He is swift as the waters; their portion is cursed in the earth: he beholdeth not the way of the vineyards.

19. Drought and heat consume the snow waters: so doth the grave those which have sinned.

20. The womb shall forget him; the worm shall feed sweetly on him; he shall be no more remembered; and wickedness shall be broken as a tree.

21. He evil entreateth the barren that beareth not: and doeth not good to the widow.

22. He draweth also the mighty with his power: he riseth up, and no man is sure of life.

23. Though it be given him to be in safety, whereon he resteth; yet his eyes are upon their ways.

24. They are exalted for a little while, but are gone and brought low; they are taken out of the way as all other, and cut off as the tops of the ears of corn.

25. And if it be not so now, who will make me a liar, and make my speech nothing worth?

CHAPTER TWENTY-FIVE

Then answered Bildad the Shuhite, and said,

2. Dominion and fear are with him, he maketh peace in his high places.

3. Is there any number of his armies? and upon whom doth not his light arise?

4. How then can man be justified with God? or how can he be clean that is born of a woman?

5. Behold even to the moon, and it shineth not; yea, the stars are not pure in his sight.

6. How much less man, that is a worm? and the son of man, which is a worm?

CHAPTER TWENTY-SIX

But Job answered and said,

2. How hast thou helped him that is without power? how savest thou the arm that hath no strength?

3. How hast thou counselled him that hath no wisdom? and how hast thou plentifully declared the thing as it is?

4. To whom hast thou uttered words? and whose spirit came from thee?

5. Dead things are formed from under the waters, and the inhabitants thereof.

6. Hell is naked before him, and destruction hath no covering.

7. He stretcheth out the north over the empty place, and hangeth the earth upon nothing.

8. He bindeth up the waters in his thick clouds; and the cloud is not rent under them.

9. He holdeth back the face of his throne, and spreadeth his cloud upon it.

10. He hath compassed the waters with bounds, until the day and night come to an end.

11. The pillars of heaven tremble and are astonished at his reproof.

12. He divideth the sea with his power, and by his understanding he smiteth through the proud.

13. By his spirit he hath garnished the heavens; his hand hath formed the crooked serpent.

14. Lo, these are parts of his ways: but how little a portion is heard of him? but the thunder of his power who can understand?

CHAPTER TWENTY-SEVEN

Moreover Job continued his parable, and said,

2. As God liveth, who hath taken away my judgment; and the Almighty, who hath vexed my soul;

3. All the while my breath is in me, and the spirit of God is in my nostrils;

4. My lips shall not speak wickedness, nor my tongue utter deceit.

5. God forbid that I should justify you: till I die I will not remove mine integrity from me.

6. My righteousness I hold fast, and will not let it go: my heart shall not reproach me so long as I live.

7. Let mine enemy be as the wicked, and he that riseth up against me as the unrighteous.

8. For what is the hope of the hypocrite, though he hath gained, when God taketh away his soul?

9. Will God hear his cry when trouble cometh upon him?

10. Will be delight himself in the Almighty? will he always call upon God?

11. I will teach you by the hand of God: that which is with the Almighty will I not conceal.

12. Behold, all ye yourselves have seen it; why then are ye thus altogether vain?

13. This is the portion of a wicked man with God, and the heritage of oppressors, which they shall receive of the Almighty.

14. If his children be multiplied, it is for the sword: and his offspring shall not be satisfied with bread.

15. Those that remain of him shall be buried in death: and his widows shall not weep.

16. Though he heap up silver as the dust, and prepare raiment as the clay;

17. He may prepare it, but the just shall put it on, and the innocent shall divide the silver.

18. He buildeth his house as a moth, and as a booth that the keeper maketh.

19. The rich man shall lie down, but he shall not be gathered: he openeth his eyes, and he is not.

20. Terrors take hold on him as waters, a tempest stealeth him away in the night.

21. The east wind carrieth him away, and he departeth: and as a storm hurleth him out of his place.

22. For God shall cast upon him, and not spare: he would fain flee out of his hand.

23. Men shall clap their hands at him, and shall hiss him out of his place.

CHAPTER TWENTY-EIGHT

Surely there is a vein for the silver, and a place for gold where they fine it.

2. Iron is taken out of the earth, and brass is molten out of the stone.

3. He setteth an end to darkness, and searcheth out all perfection: the stones of darkness, and the shadow of death.

4. The flood breaketh out from the inhabitant; even the waters forgotten of the foot: they are dried up, they are gone away from men.

5. As for the earth, out of it cometh bread: and under it is turned up as it were fire.

6. The stones of it are the place of sapphires: and it hath dust of gold.

7. There is a path which no fowl knoweth, and which the vulture's eye hath not seen:

8. The lion's whelps have not trodden it, nor the fierce lion passed by it.

9. He putteth forth his hand upon the rock; he overturneth the mountains by the roots.

10. He cutteth out rivers among the rocks; and his eye seeth every precious thing.

11. He bindeth the floods from overflowing; and the thing that is hid bringeth he forth to light.

12. But where shall wisdom be found? and where is the place of understanding?

13. Man knoweth not the price thereof; neither is it found in the land of the living.

14. The depth saith, It is not in me: and the sea saith, It is not with me.

15. It cannot be gotten for gold, neither shall silver be weighed for the price thereof.

16. It cannot be valued with the gold of Ophir, with the precious onyx, or the sapphire.

17. The gold and the crystal cannot equal it: and the exchange of it shall not be for jewels of fine gold.

18. No mention shall be made of coral, or of pearls: for the price of wisdom is above rubies.

19. The topaz of Ethiopia shall not equal it, neither shall it be valued with pure gold.

20. Whence then cometh wisdom? and where is the place of understanding?

21. Seeing it is hid from the eyes of all living, and kept close from the fowls of the air.

22. Destruction and death say, We have heard the fame thereof with our ears.

23. God understandeth the way thereof, and he knoweth the place thereof.

24. For he looketh to the ends of the earth, and seeth under the whole heaven;

25. To make the weight for the winds; and he weigheth the waters by measure.

26. When he made a decree for the rain, and a way for the lightning of the thunder:

27. Then did he see it, and declare it; he prepared it, yea, and searched it out.

28. And unto man he said, Behold, the fear of the Lord, that is wisdom; and to depart from evil is understanding.

CHAPTER TWENTY-NINE

Moreover Job continued his parable, and said,

2. Oh that I were as in months past, as in the days when God preserved me;

3. When his candle shined upon my head, and when by his light I walked through darkness;

4. As I was in the days of my youth, when the secret of God was upon my tabernacle;

5. When the Almighty was yet with me, when my children were about me;

6. When I washed my steps with butter, and the rock poured me out rivers of oil;

7. When I went out to the gate through the city, when I prepared my seat in the street!

8. The young men saw me, and hid themselves: and the aged arose, and stood up.

9. The princes refrained talking, and laid their hand on their mouth.

10. The nobles held their peace, and their tongue cleaved to the roof of their mouth.

11. When the ear heard me, then it blessed me; and when the eye saw me, it gave witness to me:

12. Because I delivered the poor that cried, and the fatherless, and him that had none to help him.

13. The blessing of him that was ready to perish came upon me: and I caused the widow's heart to sing for joy.

14. I put on righteousness, and it clothed me: my judgment was as a robe and a diadem.

15. I was eyes to the blind, and feet was I to the lame.

16. I was a father to the poor: and the cause which I knew not I searched out.

17. And I brake the jaws of the wicked, and plucked the spoil out of his teeth.

18. Then I said, I shall die in my nest, and I shall multiply my days as the sand.

19. My root was spread out by the waters, and the dew lay all night upon my branch.

20. My glory was fresh in me, and my bow was renewed in my hand.

21. Unto me men gave ear, and waited, and kept silence at my counsel.

22. After my words they spake not again; and my speech dropped upon them.

23. And they waited for me as for the rain; and they opened their mouth wide as for the latter rain.

24. If I laughed on them, they believed it not; and the light of my countenance they cast not down.

25. I chose out their way, and sat chief, and dwelt as a king in the army, as one that comforteth the mourners.

CHAPTER THIRTY

But now they that are younger than I have me in derision, whose fathers I would have disdained to have set with the dogs of my flock.

2. Yea, whereto might the strength of their hands profit me, in whom old age was perished?

3. For want and famine they were solitary; fleeing into the wilderness in former time desolate and waste.

4. Who cut up mallows by the bushes, and juniper roots for their meat.

5. They were driven forth from among men, (they cried after them as after a thief;)

6. To dwell in the clifts of the valleys, in caves of the earth, and in the rocks.

7. Among the bushes they brayed; under the nettles they were gathered together.

8. They were children of fools, yea, children of base men: they were viler than the earth.

9. And now am I their song, yea, I am their byword.

10. They abhor me, they flee far from me, and spare not to spit in my face.

11. Because he hath loosed my cord, and afflicted me, they have also let loose the bridle before me.

12. Upon my right hand rise the youth; they push away my feet, and they raise up against me the ways of their destruction.

13. They mar my path, they set forward my calamity, they have no helper.

14. They came upon me as a wide breaking in of waters: in the desolation they rolled themselves upon me.

15. Terrors are turned upon me: they pursue my soul as the wind: and my welfare passeth away as a cloud.

16. And now my soul is poured out upon me; the days of affliction have taken hold upon me.

17. My bones are pierced in me in the night season: and my sinews take no rest.

18. By the great force of my disease is my garment changed: it bindeth me about as the collar of my coat.

19. He hath cast me into the mire, and I am become like dust and ashes.

20. I cry unto thee, and thou dost not hear me: I stand up, and thou regardest me not.

21. Thou art become cruel to me: with thy strong hand thou opposest thyself against me.

22. Thou liftest me up to the wind; thou causest me to ride upon it, and dissolvest my substance.

23. For I know that thou wilt bring me to death, and to the house appointed for all living.

24. Howbeit he will not stretch out his hand to the grave, though they cry in his destruction.

25. Did not I weep for him that was in trouble? was not my soul grieved for the poor?

26. When I looked for good, then evil came unto me: and when I waited for light, there came darkness.

27. My bowels boiled, and rested not: the days of affliction prevented me.

28. I went mourning without the sun: I stood up, and I cried in the congregation.

29. I am a brother to dragons, and a companion to owls.

30. My skin is black upon me, and my bones are burned with heat.

31. My harp also is turned to mourning, and my organ into the voice of them that weep.

CHAPTER THIRTY-ONE

I made a covenant with mine eyes; why then should I think upon a maid?

2. For what portion of God is there from above? and what inheritance of the Almighty from on high?

3. Is not destruction to the wicked? and a strange punishment to the workers of iniquity?

4. Doth not he see my ways, and count all my steps?

5. If I have walked with vanity, or if my foot hath hasted to deceit;

6. Let me be weighed in an even balance, that God may know mine integrity.

7. If my step hath turned out of the way, and mine heart walked after mine eyes, and if any blot hath cleaved to mine hands;

8. Then let me sow, and let another eat; yea, let my offspring be rooted out.

9. If mine heart have been deceived by a woman, or if I have laid wait at my neighbour's door;

10. Then let my wife grind unto another, and let others bow down upon her.

11. For this is an heinous crime; yea, it is an iniquity to be punished by the judges.

12. For it is a fire that consumeth to destruction, and would root out all mine increase.

13. If I did despise the cause of my manservant or of my maidservant, when they contended with me;

14. What then shall I do when God riseth up? and when he visiteth, what shall I answer him?

15. Did not he that made me in the womb make him? and did not one fashion us in the womb?

16. If I have withheld the poor from their desire, or have caused the eyes of the widow to fail;

17. Or have eaten my morsel myself alone, and the fatherless hath not eaten thereof;

18. (For from my youth he was brought up with me, as with a father, and I have guided her from my mother's womb;)

19. If I have seen any perish for want of clothing, or any poor without covering;

20. If his loins have not blessed me, and if he were not warmed with the fleece of my sheep;

21. If I have lifted up my hand against the fatherless, when I saw my help in the gate:

22. Then let mine arm fall from my shoulder blade, and mine arm be broken from the bone.

23. For destruction from God was a terror to me, and by reason of his highness I could not endure.

24. If I have made gold my hope, or have said to the fine gold, Thou art my confidence;

25. If I rejoiced because my wealth was great, and because mine hand had gotten much;

26. If I beheld the sun when it shined, or the moon walking in brightness;

27. And my heart hath been secretly enticed, or my mouth hath kissed my hand:

28. This also were an iniquity to be punished by the judge: for I should have denied the God that is above.

29. If I rejoiced at the destruction of him that hated me, or lifted up myself when evil found him:

30. Neither have I suffered my mouth to sin by wishing a curse to his soul.

31. If the men of my tabernacle said not, Oh that we had of his flesh! we cannot be satisfied.

32. The stranger did not lodge in the street: but I opened my doors to the traveller.

33. If I covered my transgressions as Adam, by hiding mine iniquity in my bosom:

34. Did I fear a great multitude, or did the contempt of families terrify me, that I kept silence, and went not out of the door?

35. Oh that one would hear me! behold, my desire is, that the Almighty would answer me, and that mine adversary had written a book.

36. Surely I would take it upon my shoulder, and bind it as a crown to me.

37. I would declare unto him the number of my steps; as a prince would I go near unto him.

38. If my land cry against me, or that the furrows likewise thereof complain;

39. If I have eaten the fruits thereof without money, or have caused the owners thereof to lose their life:

40. Let thistles grow instead of wheat, and cockle instead of barley. The words of Job are ended.

CHAPTER THIRTY-TWO

So these three men ceased to answer Job, because he was righteous in his own eyes.

2. Then was kindled the wrath of Elihu the son of Barachel the Buzite, of the kindred of Ram: against Job was his wrath kindled, because he justified himself rather than God.

3. Also against his three friends was his wrath kindled, because they had found no answer, and yet had condemned Job.

4. Now Elihu had waited till Job had spoken, because they were elder than he.

5. When Elihu saw that there was no answer in the mouth of these three men, then his wrath was kindled.

6. And Elihu the son of Barachel the Buzite answered and said, I am young, and ye are very old; wherefore I was afraid, and durst not shew you mine opinion.

7. I said, Days should speak, and multitude of years should teach wisdom.

8. But there is a spirit in man; and the inspiration of the Almighty giveth them understanding.

9. Great men are not always wise: neither do the aged understand judgment.

10. Therefore I said, Hearken to me; I also will shew mine opinion.

11. Behold, I waited for your words; I gave ear to your reasons, whilst ye searched out what to say.

12. Yes, I attended unto you, and, behold, there was none of you that convinced Job, or that answered his words:

13. Lest ye should say, We have found out wisdom: God thrusteth him down, not man.

14. Now he hath not directed his words against me: neither will I answer him with your speeches.

15. They were amazed, they answered no more: they left off speaking.

16. When I had waited, (for they spake not, but stood still, and answered no more;)

17. I said, I will answer also my part, I also will shew mine opinion.

18. For I am full of matter, the spirit within me constraineth me.

19. Behold, my belly is as wine which hath no vent; it is ready to burst like new bottles.

20. I will speak, that I may be refreshed: I will open my lips and answer.

21. Let me not, I pray you, accept any man's person, neither let me give flattering titles unto man.

22. For I know not to give flattering titles; in so doing my maker would soon take me away.

CHAPTER THIRTY-THREE

Wherefore, Job, I pray thee, hear my speeches, and hearken to all my words.

2. Behold, now I have opened my mouth, my tongue hath spoken in my mouth.

3. My words shall be of the uprightness of my heart: and my lips shall utter knowledge clearly.

4. The Spirit of God hath made me, and the breath of the Almighty hath given me life.

5. If thou canst answer me, set thy words in order before me, stand up.

6. Behold, I am according to thy wish in God's stead: I also am formed out of the clay.

7. Behold, my terror shall not make thee afraid, neither shall my hand be heavy upon thee.

8. Surely thou hast spoken in mine hearing, and I have heard the voice of thy words, saying,

9. I am clean without transgression, I am innocent; neither is there iniquity in me.

10. Behold, he findeth occasions against me, he counteth me for his enemy,

11. He putteth my feet in the stocks, he marketh all my paths.

12. Behold, in this thou art not just: I will answer thee, that God is greater than man.

13. Why dost thou strive against him? for he giveth not account of any of his matters.

14. For God speaketh once, yea twice, yet man perceiveth it not.

15. In a dream, in a vision of the night, when deep sleep falleth upon men, in slumberings upon the bed;

16. Then he openeth the ears of men, and sealeth their instruction,

17. That he may withdraw man from his purpose, and hide pride from man.

18. He keepeth back his soul from the pit, and his life from perishing by the sword.

19. He is chastened also with pain upon his bed, and the multitude of his bones with strong pain:

20. So that his life abhorreth bread, and his soul dainty meat.

21. His flesh is consumed away, that it cannot be seen; and his bones that were not seen stick out.

22. Yes, his soul draweth near unto the grave, and his life to the destroyers.

23. If there be a messenger with him, an interpreter, one among a thousand, to shew unto man his uprightness:

24. Then he is gracious unto him, and saith, Deliver him from going down to the pit: I have found a ransom.

25. His flesh shall be fresher than a child's: he shall return to the days of his youth:

26. He shall pray unto God, and he will be favourable unto him: and he shall see his face with joy: for he will render unto man his righteousness.

27. He looketh upon men, and if any say, I have sinned, and perverted that which was right, and it profited me not;

28. He will deliver his soul from going into the pit, and his life shall see the light.

29. Lo, all these things worketh God oftentimes with man,

30. To bring back his soul from the pit, to be enlightened with the light of the living.

31. Mark well, O Job, hearken unto me: hold thy peace, and I will speak.

32. If thou hast any thing to say, answer me: speak, for I desire to justify thee.

33. If not, hearken unto me: hold thy peace, and I shall teach thee wisdom.

CHAPTER THIRTY-FOUR

Furthermore Elihu answered and said,

2. Hear my words, O ye wise men; and give ear unto me, ye that have knowledge.

3. For the ear trieth words, as the mouth tasteth meat.

4. Let us choose to us judgment: let us know among ourselves what is good.

5. For Job hath said, I am righteous: and God hath taken away my judgment.

6. Should I lie against my right? my wound is incurable without transgression.

7. What man is like Job, who drinketh up scorning like water?

8. Which goeth in company with the workers of iniquity, and walketh with wicked men.

9. For he hath said, It profiteth a man nothing that he should delight himself with God.

10. Therefore hearken unto me, ye men of understanding: far be it from God, that he should do wickedness; and from the Almighty, that he should commit iniquity.

11. For the work of a man shall he render unto him, and cause every man to find according to his ways.

12. Yea, surely God will not do wickedly, neither will the Almighty pervert judgment.

13. Who hath given him a charge over the earth? or who hath disposed the whole world?

14. If he set his heart upon man, if he gather unto himself his spirit and his breath;

15. All flesh shall perish together, and man shall turn again unto dust.

16. If now thou hast understanding, hear this: hearken to the voice of my words.

17. Shall even he that hateth right govern? and wilt thou condemn him that is most just?

18. Is it fit to say to a king, Thou art wicked? and to princes, Ye are ungodly?

19. How much less to him that accepteth not the persons of princes, nor regardeth the rich more than the poor? for they all are the work of his hands.

20. In a moment shall they die, and the people shall be troubled at midnight, and pass away: and the mighty shall be taken away without hand.

21. For his eyes are upon the ways of man, and he seeth all his goings.

22. There is no darkness, nor shadow of death, where the workers of iniquity may hide themselves.

23. For he will not lay upon man more than right; that he should enter into judgment with God.

24. He shall break in pieces mighty men without number, and set others in their stead.

25. Therefore he knoweth their works, and he overturneth them in the night, so that they are destroyed.

26. He striketh them as wicked men in the open sight of others;

27. Because they turned back from him, and would not consider any of his ways:

28. So that they cause the cry of the poor to come unto him, and he heareth the cry of the afflicted.

29. When he giveth quietness, who then can make trouble? and when he hideth his face, who then can behold him? whether it be done against a nation, or against a man only:

30. That the hypocrite reign not, lest the people be ensnared.

31. Surely it is meet to be said unto God, I have borne chastisement, I will not offend any more:

32. That which I see not teach thou me: if I have done iniquity, I will do no more.

33. Should it be according to thy mind? he will recompense it, whether thou refuse, or whether thou choose; and not I: therefore speak what thou knowest.

34. Let men of understanding tell me, and let a wise man hearken unto me.

35. Job hath spoken without knowledge, and his words were without wisdom.

36. My desire is that Job may be tried unto the end because of his answers for wicked men.

37. For he addeth rebellion unto his sin, he clappeth his hands among us, and multiplieth his words against God.

CHAPTER THIRTY-FIVE

Elihu spake moreover, and said,

2. Thinkest thou this to be right, that thou saidst, My righteousness is more than God's?

3. For thou saidst, What advantage will it be unto thee? and, What profit shall I have, if I be cleansed from my sin?

4. I will answer thee, and thy companions with thee.

5. Look unto the heavens, and see; and behold the clouds which are higher than thou.

6. If thou sinnest, what doest thou against him? of if thy transgressions be multiplied, what doest thou unto him?

7. If thou be righteous, what givest thou him? or what receiveth he of thine hand?

8. Thy wickedness may hurt a man as thou art; and thy righteousness may profit the son of man.

9. By reason of the multitude of oppressions they make the oppressed to cry: they cry out by reason of the arm of the mighty.

10. But none saith, Where is God my maker, who giveth songs in the night;

11. Who teacheth us more than the beasts of the earth, and maketh us wiser than the fowls of heaven?

12. There they cry, but none giveth answer, because of the pride of evil men.

13. Surely God will not hear vanity, neither will the Almighty regard it.

14. Although thou sayest thou shalt not see him, yet judgment is before him; therefore trust thou in him.

15. But now, because it is not so, he hath visited in his anger; yet he knoweth it not in great extremity:

16. Therefore doth Job open his mouth in vain; he multiplieth words without knowledge.

CHAPTER THIRTY-SIX

Elihu also proceeded, and said,

2. Suffer me a little, and I will shew thee that I have yet to speak on God's behalf.

3. I will fetch my knowledge from afar, and will ascribe righteousness to my Maker.

4. For truly my words shall not be false: he that is perfect in knowledge is with thee.

5. Behold, God is mighty, and despiseth not any: he is mighty in strength and wisdom.

6. He preserveth not the life of the wicked: but giveth right to the poor.

7. He withdraweth not his eyes from the righteous: but with kings are they on the throne; yea, he doth establish them for ever, and they are exalted.

8. And if they be bound in fetters, and be holden in cords of affliction;

9. Then he sheweth them their work, and their transgressions that they have exceeded.

10. He openeth also their ear to discipline, and commandeth that they return from iniquity.

11. If they obey and serve him, they shall spend their days in prosperity, and their years in pleasures.

12. But if they obey not, they shall perish by the sword, and they shall die without knowledge.

13. But the hypocrites in heart heap up wrath: they cry not when he bindeth them.

14. They die in youth, and their life is among the unclean.

15. He delivereth the poor in his affliction, and openeth their ears in oppression.

16. Even so would he have removed thee out of the strait into a broad place, where there is no straitness; and that which should be set on thy table should be full of fatness.

17. But thou hast fulfilled the judgment of the wicked: judgment and justice take hold on thee.

18. Because there is wrath, beware lest he take thee away with his stroke: then a great ransom cannot deliver thee.

19. Will he esteem thy riches? no, not gold, nor all the forces of strength.

20. Desire not the night, when people are cut off in their place.

21. Take heed, regard not iniquity: for this hast thou chosen rather than affliction.

22. Behold, God exalteth by his power: who teacheth like him?

23. Who hath enjoined him his way? or who can say, Thou hast wrought iniquity?

24. Remember that thou magnify his work, which men behold.

25. Every man may see it; man may behold it afar off.

26. Behold, God is great, and we know him not, neither can the number of his years be searched out.

27. For he maketh small the drops of water: they pour down rain according to the vapour thereof:

28. Which the clouds do drop and distil upon man abundantly.

29. Also can any understand the spreadings of the clouds, or the noise of his tabernacle?

30. Behold, he spreadeth his light upon it, and covereth the bottom of the sea.

31. For by them judgeth he the people; he giveth meat in abundance.

32. With clouds he covereth the light; and commandeth it not to shine by the cloud that cometh betwixt.

33. The noise thereof sheweth concerning it, the cattle also concerning the vapour.

CHAPTER THIRTY-SEVEN

At this also my heart trembleth, and is moved out of his place.

2. Hear attentively the noise of his voice, and the sound that goeth out of his mouth.

3. He directeth it under the whole heaven, and his lightning unto the ends of the earth.

4. After it a voice roareth: he thundereth with the voice of his excellency; and he will not stay them when his voice is heard.

5. God thundereth marvellously with his voice; great things doeth he, which we cannot comprehend.

6. For he saith to the snow, Be thou on the earth; likewise to the small rain, and to the great rain of his strength.

7. He sealeth up the hand of every man; that all men may know his work.

8. Then the beasts go into dens, and remain in their places.

9. Out of the south cometh the whirlwind: and cold out of the north.

10. By the breath of God frost is given: and the breadth of the waters is straitened.

11. Also by watering he wearieth the thick cloud: he scattereth his bright cloud:

12. And it is turned round about by his counsels: that they may do whatsoever he commandeth them upon the face of the world in the earth.

13. He causeth it to come, whether for correction, or for his land, or for mercy.

14. Hearken unto this, O Job: stand still, and consider the wondrous works of God.

15. Dost thou know when God disposed them, and caused the light of his cloud to shine?

16. Dost thou know the balancings of the clouds, the wondrous works of him which is perfect in knowledge?

17. How thy garments are warm, when he quieteth the earth by the south wind?

18. Hast thou with him spread out the sky, which is strong, and as a molten looking glass?

19. Teach us what we shall say unto him; for we cannot order our speech by reason of darkness.

20. Shall it be told him that I speak? if a man speak, surely he shall be swallowed up.

21. And now men see not the bright light which is in the clouds: but the wind passeth, and cleanseth them.

22. Fair weather cometh out of the north: with God is terrible majesty.

23. Touching the Almighty, we cannot find him out: he is excellent in power, and in judgment, and in plenty of justice: he will not afflict.

24. Men do therefore fear him: he respecteth not any that are wise of heart.

CHAPTER THIRTY-EIGHT

Then the Lord answered Job out of the whirlwind, and said,

2. Who is this that darkeneth counsel by words without knowledge?

3. Gird up now thy loins like a man; for I will demand of thee, and answer thou me.

4. Where wast thou when I laid the foundations of the earth? declare, if thou hast understanding.

5. Who hath laid the measures thereof, if thou knowest? or who hath stretched the line upon it?

6. Whereupon are the foundations thereof fastened? or who laid the corner stone thereof;

7. When the morning stars sang together, and all the sons of God shouted for joy?

8. Or who shut up the sea with doors, when it brake forth, as if it had issued out of the womb?

9. When I made the cloud the garment thereof, and thick darkness a swaddlingband for it,

10. And brake up for it my decreed place, and set bars and doors,

11. And said, Hitherto shalt thou come, but no further: and here shall thy proud waves be stayed?

12. Hast thou commanded the morning since thy days; and caused the dayspring to know his place;

13. That it might take hold of the ends of the earth, that the wicked might be shaken out of it?

14. It is turned as clay to the seal; and they stand as a garment.

15. And from the wicked their light is withholden, and the high arm shall be broken.

16. Hast thou entered into the springs of the sea? or hast thou walked in the search of the depth?

17. Have the gates of death been opened unto thee? or hast thou seen the doors of the shadow of death?

18. Hast thou perceived the breadth of the earth? declare if thou knowest it all.

19. Where is the way where light dwelleth? and as for darkness, where is the place thereof,

20. That thou shouldest take it to the bound thereof, and that thou shouldest know the paths to the house thereof?

21. Knowest thou it, because thou wast then born? or because the number of thy days is great?

22. Hast thou entered into the treasures of the snow? or hast thou seen the treasures of the hail,

23. Which I have reserved against the time of trouble, against the day of battle and war?

24. By what way is the light parted, which scattereth the east wind upon the earth?

25. Who hath divided a watercourse for the overflowing of waters, or a way for the lightning of thunder;

26. To cause it to rain on the earth, where no man is; on the wilderness, wherein there is no man;

27. To satisfy the desolate and waste ground; and to cause the bud of the tender herb to spring forth?

28. Hath the rain a father? or who hath begotten the drops of dew?

29. Out of whose womb came the ice? and the hoary frost of heaven, who hath gendered it?

30. The waters are hid as with a stone, and the face of the deep is frozen.

31. Canst thou bind the sweet influences of Pleiades, or loose the bands of Orion?

32. Canst thou bring forth Mazzaroth in his season? or canst thou guide Arcturus with his sons?

33. Knowest thou the ordinances of heaven? canst thou set the dominion thereof in the earth?

34. Canst thou lift up thy voice to the clouds, that abundance of waters may cover thee?

35. Canst thou send lightnings, that they may go, and say unto thee, Here we are?

36. Who hath put wisdom in the inward parts? or who hath given understanding to the heart?

37. Who can number the clouds in wisdom? or who can stay the bottles of heaven,

38. When the dust groweth into hardness, and the clods cleave fast together?

39. Wilt thou hunt the prey for the lion? or fill the appetite of the young lions,

40. When they couch in their dens, and abide in the covert to lie in wait?

41. Who provideth for the raven his food? when his young ones cry unto God, they wander for lack of meat.

CHAPTER THIRTY-NINE

Knowest thou the time when the wild goats of the rock bring forth? or canst thou mark when the hinds do calve?

2. Canst thou number the months that they fulfil? or knowest thou the time when they bring forth?

3. They bow themselves, they bring forth their young ones, they cast out their sorrows.

4. Their young ones are in good liking, they grow up with corn; they go forth, and return not unto them.

5. Who hath sent out the wild ass free? or who hath loosed the bands of the wild ass?

6. Whose house I have made the wilderness, and the barren land his dwellings.

7. He scorneth the multitude of the city, neither regardeth he the crying of the driver.

8. The range of the mountains is his pasture, and he searcheth after every green thing.

9. Will the unicorn be willing to serve thee, or abide by thy crib?

10. Canst thou bind the unicorn with his band in the furrow? or will he harrow the valleys after thee?

11. Wilt thou trust him, because his strength is great? or wilt thou leave thy labour to him?

12. Wilt thou believe him, that he will bring home thy seed, and gather it into thy barn?

13. Gavest thou the goodly wings unto the peacocks? or wings and feathers unto the ostrich?

14. Which leaveth her eggs in the earth, and warmeth them in dust,

15. And forgetteth that the foot may crush them, or that the wild beast may break them.

16. She is hardened against her young ones, as though they were not hers: her labour is in vain without fear;

17. Because God hath deprived her of wisdom, neither hath he imparted to her understanding.

18. What time she lifteth up her self on high, she scorneth the horse and his rider.

19. Hast thou given the horse strength? hast thou clothed his neck with thunder?

20. Canst thou make him afraid as a grasshopper? the glory of his nostrils is terrible.

21. He paweth in the valley, and rejoiceth in his strength: he goeth on to meet the armed men.

22. He mocketh at fear, and is not affrighted; neither turneth he back from the sword.

23. The quiver rattleth against him, the glittering spear and the shield.

24. He swalloweth the ground with fierceness and rage: neither believeth he that it is the sound of the trumpet.

25. He saith among the trumpets, Ha, ha; and he smelleth the battle afar off, the thunder of the captains, and the shouting.

26. Doth the hawk fly by thy wisdom, and stretch her wings toward the south?

27. Doth the eagle mount up at thy command, and make her nest on high?

28. She dwelleth and abideth on the rock, upon the crag of the rock, and the strong place.

29. From thence she seeketh the prey, and her eyes behold afar off.

30. Her young ones also suck up blood: and where the slain are, there is she.

CHAPTER FORTY

Moreover the LORD answered Job, and said,

2. Shall he that contendeth with the Almighty instruct him? he that reproveth God, let him answer it.

3. ¶Then Job answered the LORD, and said,

4. Behold, I am vile; what shall I answer thee? I will lay mine hand upon my mouth.

5. Once have I spoken; but I will not answer: yea, twice; but I will proceed no further.

6. ¶Then answered the LORD unto Job out of the whirlwind, and said,

7. Gird up thy loins now like a man: I will demand of thee, and declare thou unto me.

8. Wilt thou also disannul my judgment? wilt thou condemn me, that thou mayest be righteous?

9. Hast thou an arm like God? or canst thou thunder with a voice like him?

10. Deck thyself now with majesty and excellency; and array thyself with glory and beauty.

11. Cast abroad the rage of thy wrath: and behold every one that is proud, and abase him.

12. Look on every one that is proud, and bring him low; and tread down the wicked in their place.

13. Hide them in the dust together; and bind their faces in secret.

14. Then will I also confess unto thee that thine own right hand can save thee.

15. ¶Behold now behemoth, which I made with thee; he eateth grass as an ox.

16. Lo now, his strength is in his loins, and his force is in the navel of his belly.

17. He moveth his tail like a cedar: the sinews of his stones are wrapped together.

18. His bones are as strong pieces of brass; his bones are like bars of iron.

19. He is the chief of the ways of God: he that made him can make his sword to approach unto him.

20. Surely the mountains bring him forth food, where all the beasts of the field play.

21. He lieth under the shady trees, in the covert of the reed, and fens.

22. The shady trees cover him with their shadow; the willows of the brook compass him about.

23. Behold, he drinketh up a river, and hasteth not: he trusteth that he can draw up Jordan into his mouth.

24. He taketh it with his eyes: his nose pierceth through snares.

CHAPTER FORTY-ONE

Canst thou draw out leviathan with an hook? or his tongue with a cord which thou lettest down?

2. Canst thou put an hook into his nose? or bore his jaw through with a thorn?

3. Will he make many supplications unto thee? will he speak soft words unto thee?

4. Will he make a covenant with thee? wilt thou take him for a servant for ever?

5. Wilt thou play with him as with a bird? or wilt thou bind him for thy maidens?

6. Shall the companions make a banquet of him? shall they part him among the merchants?

7. Canst thou fill his skin with barbed irons? or his head with fish spears?

8. Lay thine hand upon him, remember the battle, do no more.

9. Behold, the hope of him is in vain: shall not one be cast down even at the sight of him?

10. None is so fierce that dare stir him up: who then is able to stand before me?

11. Who hath prevented me, that I should repay him? whatsoever is under the whole heaven is mine.

12. I will not conceal his parts, nor his power, nor his comely proportion.

13. Who can discover the face of his garment? or who can come to him with his double bridle?

14. Who can open the doors of his face? his teeth are terrible round about.

15. His scales are his pride, shut up together as with a close seal.

16. One is so near to another, that no air can come between them.

17. They are joined one to another, they stick together, that they cannot be sundered.

18. By his neesings a light doth shine, and his eyes are like the eyelids of the morning.

19. Out of his mouth go burning lamps, and sparks of fire leap out.

20. Out of his nostrils goeth smoke, as out of a seething pot or caldron.

21. His breath kindleth coals, and a flame goeth out of his mouth.

22. In his neck remaineth strength, and sorrow is turned into joy before him.

23. The flakes of his flesh are joined together: they are firm in themselves; they cannot be moved.

24. His heart is as firm as a stone; yea, as hard as a piece of the nether millstone.

25. When he raiseth up himself, the mighty are afraid: by reason of breakings they purify themselves.

26. The sword of him that layeth at him cannot hold: the spear, the dart, nor the habergeon.

27. He esteemeth iron as straw, and brass as rotten wood.

28. The arrow cannot make him flee: alingstones are turned with him into stubble.

29. Darts are counted as stubble: he laugheth at the shaking of a spear.

30. Sharp stones are under him: he spreadeth sharp pointed things upon the mire.

31. He maketh the deep to boil like a pot: he maketh the sea like a pot of ointment.

32. He maketh a path to shine after him; one would think the deep to be hoary.

33. Upon earth there is not his like, who is made without fear.

34. He beholdeth all high things: he is a king over all the children of pride.

CHAPTER FORTY-TWO

Then Job answered the LORD, and said,

2. I know that thou canst do every thing, and that no thought can be withholden from thee.

3. Who is he that hideth counsel without knowledge? therefore have I uttered that I understood not; things too wonderful for me, which I knew not.

4. Hear, I beseech thee, and I will speak: I will demand of thee, and declare thou unto me.

5. I have heard of thee by the hearing of the ear: but now mine eye seeth thee.

6. Wherefore I abhor myself, and repent in dust and ashes.

7. ¶And it was so, that after the LORD had spoken these words unto Job, the LORD said to Eliphaz the Temanite, My wrath is kindled against thee, and against thy two friends: for ye have not spoken of me the thing that is right, as my servant Job hath.

8. Therefore take unto you now seven bullocks and seven rams, and go to my servant Job, and offer up for yourselves a burnt offering; and my servant Job shall pray for you: for him will I accept: lest I deal with you after your folly, in that

ye have not spoken of me the thing which is right, like my servant Job.

9. So Eliphaz the Temanite and Bildad the Shuhite and Zophar the Naamathite went, and did according as the LORD commanded them: the LORD also accepted Job.

10. And the LORD turned the captivity of Job, when he prayed for his friends: also the LORD gave Job twice as much as he had before.

11. Then came there unto him all his brethren, and all his sisters, and all they that had been of his acquaintance before, and did eat bread with him in his house: and they bemoaned him, and comforted him over all the evil that the LORD had brought upon him: every man also gave him a piece of money, and every one an earring of gold.

12. So the LORD blessed the latter end of Job more than his beginning: for he had fourteen thousand sheep, and six thousand camels, and a thousand yoke of oxen, and a thousand she asses.

13. He had also seven sons and three daughters.

14. And he called the name of the first, Jemima; and the name of the second, Kezia; and the name of the third, Kerenhappuch.

15. And in all the land were no women found so fair as the daughters of Job: and their father gave them inheritance among their brethren.

16. After this lived Job an hundred and forty years, and saw his sons, and his sons' sons, even four generations.

17. So Job died, being old and full of days.

Thomas Moore is the *New York Times* bestselling author of *Care of the Soul, Soul Mates, The Re-Enchantment of Everyday Life,* and many other works. He lectures on mythology and the arts in the U.S. and abroad. He lived as a monk in a Catholic religious order for twelve years, and has degrees in theology, musicology, and philosophy.